When a Pastor Search Committee Comes... or Doesn't

J. William Harbin

Foreword by Joe R. Stacker

BROADMAN PRESS
Nashville, Tennessee

TO

My wife, Marilyn

Who for thirty years as an ideal
pastor's wife gave me inspiration,
guidance, and understanding
as I sought
God's will in dealing with
Pastor Search Committees

And to

my two sons,

Bill, Jr., who this year wrote
and had published a
book in his own area of work

and to

Ben, my younger son, who suggested
and encouraged the
publishing of this work

© Copyright 1985 • Broadman Press
All rights reserved
4225-45
ISBN: 0-8054-2545-4

Dewey Decimal Classification: 253
Subject Headings: MINISTERS // PASTOR SEARCH COMMITTEE
Library of Congress Catalog Card Number: 85-13541

Printed in the United States of America

Library of Congress Cataloging-in-Publication Data

Harbin, J. William, 1922-
  When a pastor search committee comes . . . or doesn't.

  Bibliography: p.
  1. Clergy—Appointment, call, and election.
2. Pastoral search committees. I. Title.
BV664.H37 1985   262'.14   85-13541
ISBN 0-8054-2545-4 (pbk.)

Contents

Foreword 5

Preface 8

Introduction 9

Part 1
When a Pastor Search Committee Does Come

1 How to Be Prepared for a Pastor Search Committee 15

2 Getting a Pastor Search Committee to Visit and/or Hear
You Preach 23

3 When a Committee Contacts You 37

4 When a Committee Actually Visits You and Hears You
Preach 41

5 How Should You Conduct Yourself When a Committee
Interviews You? 45

6 How Can You Tell When It Is Time to Move?............... 49

7 What Should a Pastor Tell the Present Congregation or
Deacons When He Preaches at Another Church in View
of a Call?.. 59

8 The Church's Expectations of the Pastor 63

9 The Pastor's Expectations of the Church 71

10 When a Pastor Search Committee Invites and Presents
You to Its Church in View of a Call................................. 77

11 How Can You Tell When or If It Is the Right Church for
You?.. 85

12 Voting on the Prospective Pastor.. 91
13 Resignation and Closure at the Present Church 95
14 Pastorium or Housing Allowance 99
15 Getting a Good Start at the Next Pastorate...................... 105
16 An Installation Service at the New Pastorate.................... 107

Part 2
When a Pastor Search Committee Doesn't Come

17 What Does a Pastor Do When He Is Not Contacted by
    Another Church? 113
        The Pastor Who Is Having a Good Ministry
        The Pastor Who Is Having Conflict

Part 3
**When a Pastor Doesn't Want a Pastor Search Committee to
Come**

18 The Secret or Recipe for a Successful Long Pastorate 127
Conclusion 135
Notes 141
Bibliography 143

Foreword

The news of another pastor forced to leave his church causes one to wonder what is going on. Such events are debilitating. The divorce of pastor and people is shocking. Recent research in one denomination indicated that an average of eighty-eight ministers per month were being forced to terminate their leadership position. When a church goes through such an experience, it is like a death in the family. This cycle of grief is no stranger to many pastors and churches.

Churches experiencing the forced termination of a minister often suffer the departure of active church members hurt by the events of ridding the church of an unwanted pastor. This can cause a decline in membership, financial support, and vision for the future. The morale of the church is broken and the fellowship divided. When the church finds a man willing to come and serve as a new pastor, he is often unaware of the hard time he will have to pull such a church together. To recapture the sense of God's will in the life of such brokenness is quite difficult. To deal successfully with the pastor/church struggle, positive actions are needed—actions which call for the reeducation of pastors and churches on how to call a pastor. The need to know where to begin and how to proceed is critical. Books on the call to ministry are numerous. These have dealt with the biblical, theological, and philosophical nature of the call experience. The call of God and the call to a church are uniquely joined together. This must be understood by both pastor and people. The lack of awareness of how a pastor and church should come together can be the source of many problems.

J. William Harbin, out of thirty-five years in the pastorate, has written a practical guide for churches and pastors to use in the call experience. What a pastor does as he deals with a pastor search committee is most important. Appearance, family, the style of his resumé, the approaches he takes with the committee, how he uses opportunities and builds relationships with that interested church and the one which he is presently serving are a few of the items covered in this book.

The chapters on the church's expectation of the pastor and the pastor's expectation of the church are worth the cost of the book. Bill Harbin warns that a church or a pastor may miss the will of God when they don't use proven and effective methods in the call process. The content of the book seeks to answer three questions. What shall I do

when a pastor search committee does come?

when a pastor search committee doesn't come?

when I don't want a pastor search committee to come?

The answers to these questions are honest, positive, and deal with the critical issue of the leadership of God's Spirit in any and all decisions.

In pastoral leadership there are three stages; entrance, transition, and exit. It is a known fact that the transition and exit go much better when the entrance is done well. Bill Harbin's suggestions will help that entrance and thus the life of the church and the pastor as they serve together the cause of Jesus Christ. Harbin calls for an open sharing in the seeking and calling of a pastor to a church.

I recommend the good works of my friend, teacher, and brother in Christ as you seek a good entrance into ministry as a pastor and as a church. These words can make a difference in how pastors and churches get along as they share their call to ministry. May God bless your shared ministry.

JOE R. STACKER, *Secretary*
Church Administration Department
Baptist Sunday School Board

Acknowledgments

Many people have contributed to the writing of this book. I am grateful to: the church people I have pastored through these years in the ministry; the various pastor search committees I have met with since assuming my present position in 1976; the pastors who have influenced my life and ministry; and, of course, the professors at Furman University during my college days and the faculty at the Southern Baptist Theological Seminary where I spent six and one-half years in study for ministry.

I gratefully acknowledge the encouragement and help I have received from my fellow state church-minister relations group in the Southern Baptist Convention. I am also indebted to Dr. Brooks Faulkner and those from the Baptist Sunday School Board who have helped in our semiannual meetings over the years, as well as the representatives of our theological seminaries in my own denomination who have been most helpful when I visit their campuses to interview graduating students.

I express my thanks to the people at the Executive Board Building of the Tennessee Baptist Convention for their inspiration and fellowship during these years in denominational work.

My special thanks go to Mrs. Evelyn Smith, my faithful secretary and co-worker for the past nine years, who typed the manuscript and offered helpful suggestions. Also, I express thanks to my other faithful secretary and co-worker, Mrs. Sarah Bottom, who proofread the manuscript.

I would be remiss if I did not thank my wife, Marilyn, for listening to my thoughts about this work even before they materialized. Her love and encouragement have blessed my ministry through the years.

Preface

When Dr. Harbin invited me to review his book, *When a Pastor Search Committee Comes . . . or Doesn't,* I thought I would read a couple of chapters and then finish reading the book over a period of time. However, I immediately became engrossed in it and could scarcely place the manuscript down until I finished reading it.

Dr. Harbin has combined many experiences to produce this much-needed and certainly helpful book. He uses the experiences of his many years as a successful pastor. During those years he dealt with several pastor search committees, and now for nearly a decade, he has been meeting with and giving counsel to search committees seeking his help in finding God's will for the person to become pastor of their church. These experiences, along with counseling pastors and staff persons who were dealing with church members, have been focused into a most readable and helpful volume. The chapter dealing with the experiences of a pastor leaving a field was of unusual significance. Before this I have never seen anything written in this area.

I believe every person beginning his ministry would do well to read the book and will surely profit by it. Those of us who are older will not only receive help, but will read it with great delight and will recall many recollections of past experiences. I enthusiastically endorse and recommend *When a Pastor Search Committee Comes . . . or Doesn't.*

TOM MADDEN
Executive Secretary-Treasurer
Tennessee Baptist Convention

Introduction

Sometime in the life of the average minister in a church with an "open" or "restricted-open" method[1] of calling a pastor, the pastor is going to deal with a pastor search committee. The committee may call by phone before visiting the church of the minister, or the pastor may look out in the congregation some Sunday and see a group of unfamiliar people and surmise, *That's a pastor search committee.* After the worship hour is over, these people may suddenly disappear without speaking to the pastor; still again they may ask, "Could we meet with you a few minutes after everybody has gone?"

How do you answer if these people approach you and announce, "We are members of the East Church Pastor Search Committee, and we want to talk with you"?

How do you act? What do you say? How far do you go if they are interested in your coming to their church to preach a "trial sermon"? If they seem interested in you, how much interest should you reveal? Would you be willing to leave your church even if you did not want to leave? How can you tell if it is the right church for you? Would you be willing to go to a larger church or a smaller church? If you find out that the church is divided, what would be your reaction? What questions do you expect them to ask you? What questions do you want to ask them?

I am not presumptuous enough even to imagine that one minister could be wise enough, or even foolish enough, to direct another person in the ministry how to deal specifically with a pastor search committee. I am well aware of at least three facts along this line:

First, there never will be two ministers exactly alike. Consequently, no two ministers would approach the matter of dealing with a pastor search committee in the same manner or style. Some rigid or canned set of rules would destroy each minister's individuality.

Second, there will never be two pastor search committees just alike. So a helpful set of rules for one committee might be detrimental to another.

Third, and most important, an individual's opinions or suggestions can never in any form or fashion become a substitute for the leadership of the Holy Spirit. A minister who puts any person, method, or set of suggestions ahead of the Holy Spirit's leadership in dealing with a pastor search committee will be doomed to failure even if he "gets that church."

Keeping these facts in mind, the question may well be asked: Then, why spend so much time, space, and energy trying to give a few suggestions? My answer is: I believe God put a burden on my heart to help pastors deal with pastor search committees. I recall how one pastor went to a rather large church one Sunday to preach trial sermons. At the close of the evening worship hour, the church voted unanimously to call him as their pastor, and they equated their call with his acceptance. But three weeks later he was struggling for a decision. He phoned and asked if I could talk with him. I gave him a little booklet I use with pastor search committees. In that material, I state that "a church should vote on a pastor *only* after he gives his approval and is almost 100 percent sure he would accept the call if the vast majority of the votes cast are in his favor and in keeping with the policies of the church."

He said, "I would have given anything if I could have read that material before I let them vote on me." He did *not* equate the church's vote with his acceptance. He was a burdened pastor, in the throes of trying to make a decision "to go or stay." He finally rejected the call of the church after four weeks. Both the prospective pastor and the church were disappointed.

A number of seminary students (I visit four or five seminaries annually to interview students) and pastors have asked me several questions relative to dealing with pastor search committees. It's an important part of a pastor's ministry. I felt more material should be available to answer many of the questions about such a vital phase of a pastor's life.

God used the virgin Mary as a human instrument to give birth to His own Son in human flesh. One of the remarkable facts about the incarnation was that God used an orderly process of timing in sending His Son to earth because He came "in the fulness of the time" (Gal. 4:4).

I personally believe a pastor and a church should establish a relationship in an orderly fashion. A quick courtship of a pastor and pastor search committee often leads to a quick divorce, and I believe there are too many of these church and pastor divorces.

It is perfectly normal for the Holy Spirit to use some orderly principles and procedures to get a certain pastor and a certain church together. I do not think any pastor comes together with any church by sheer accident. That is why I feel some suggestions for pastors dealing with pastor search committees need to be verbalized. If such suggestions can help even one pastor or one church establish a happy relationship, I will feel amply rewarded. If Jesus Christ can be magnified by such a relationship, I will rejoice in the Lord.

That is what this book is about—to help my fellow pastors deal with pastor search committees. I do not have any intentions, or even desires, of making this book a scholarly approach about how to secure a pastorate. I merely seek to offer practical suggestions in guiding ministers to a better approach of dealing with committees and churches.

Part 1
When a Pastor Search
Committee Does Come

In this first section, I want to present practical suggestions about how a pastor can prepare for a pastor search committee that contacts him. The committee may invite him to meet with them at a specific location to have an informal "get together" for the purpose of getting to know him. If they feel impressed to do so after such a meeting, they may make arrangements to hear the pastor preach in his own church. At a later time, the same committee may want the pastor to preach in their church in view of a call.

In a few cases, the committee may do the first two things above, and then, with much investigation on the part of the committee and prospective pastor, and with several conferences between the two, he may be called as pastor of the church without the typical "trial sermon" in their own church building in view of a call.

How can a pastor prepare for such a committee? Or how can a minister get such a committee to visit and/or hear him? What procedures should you follow when a committee does show interest in you? Can you tell when it is time to leave your present situation? What should you expect from them? What do they have a right to expect of you?

I hope to give satisfactory answers to these and other questions. I also could hope these principles and procedures for dealing with a pastor search committee will help the minister in his present or next pastorate.

1

How to Be Prepared for a Pastor Search Committee

All of us are familiar with the old song, "If I Knew You Were Coming, I'd a Baked a Cake"—I would have been better prepared, in other words. And many pastors would readily admit that if they had known a pastor search committee were coming, they would have had more in the "pantry" too.

Is it possible in our "fast-food age" for the pastor to serve a nutritious spiritual dish every Sunday to unexpected guests, as well as to the regular family members? Can he continually demonstrate the "fruit of the Spirit," even when he is constantly compelled to deal with the "lusts of the flesh" among many carnal church members? Can he radiate the love of God in his messages and in his demeanor when it would be easier to succumb to the temptation of letting anger and retaliation dominate his ministry? Can your members tell you enjoy your ministry among them? Is there something about your spirit and your enthusiasm for the Lord that is contagious, and people enjoy hearing you and being around you? In other words, can you always be prepared for an unexpected or expected pastor search committee? Suppose you had a committee visit you this Sunday: Would you be ready?

Let me suggest seven vital things you can be and do to prepare:

1. Go to the pulpit every time with great expectations in your mind and heart. Expect something good to happen whenever you preach God's Word. Early in my ministry, I read about the young man who came to Charles Haddon Spurgeon, the powerful English preacher, and remarked, "Brother Spurgeon, I preach Sunday after Sunday, and nobody comes forward to make a decision for Christ." When the great pulpiteer asked, "Young man, you do not expect someone to come every Sunday, do you?" the young man replied, "Well, no, not every Sunday." The dynamic man of God then observed, "That is why they do not come."

Pastor, you may have many dry Sundays without a public decision for Christ. But keep expecting people to be saved; keep praying for spiritual growth among your members. Realize that God's Word does not return to Him void: it does accomplish its purpose when proclaimed. The seed must be sown before the harvest can be reaped, and the pastor must not have a negative attitude about God's Word and work. Decisions are being made that may not be visible immediately, but expect God to touch hearts, change lives, enrich the soul, enlighten the mind, and dispel the darkness of sin and ignorance.

I have a feeling that a pastor search committee can sense when a pastor means business for God and expects results. A committee may not always know what they want in a pastor. In fact, they may want too much in a man. They may be guilty of looking too much on the outward appearance. They may judge a person's ability and record by the statistics of the church he pastors. But a committee deeply committed to Jesus Christ cannot fail to feel a pastor's eagerness and deep concern for the spiritual welfare of his listening congregation. Pastors that display a spirit of apathy and indifference in their preaching and invitation time will not generate much power for God.

Dr. Tom Madden related the story of a young man who lived in South America. He moved to the United States but told his family he would return home someday. On the day he came home, he was standing on the deck of the ship looking at the people waiting for the passengers. Suddenly he exclaimed, "That's my dad! Who told him I was coming?" The captain of the ship replied, "No one told him you were coming. He meets this ship everytime it comes in. He said, 'One day my boy is going to be on that ship.' " That is how we ought to enter the pulpit, expecting some Jimmy or Mary to be saved or knowing that God is going to bless His Word. And when that pastor search committee does come, God's servant will be ready.

2. Stay "prayed up" every single day of your ministry. Too many pastors wait until they get under pressure to leave their churches and then initiate a campaign of prayer for God to move them.

God's Word says, "Pray without ceasing" (1 Thess. 5:17). This means to stay in an attitude of prayer. I believe God honors and respects the undershepherd who keeps a "hot line" to God more than when he calls on God simply in times of dire emergency.

When the anointed evangelist Dwight L. Moody was crossing the ocean to preach in one of his meetings, the ship on which he was sailing caught fire. When he joined the bucket brigade to help put out the fire, one of the men suggested, "Mr. Moody, let's stop and pray." Moody kept passing the buckets of water and replied, "I stay prayed up." This is a must for the man who is called to be a pastor.

One of the dangers we must avoid in our praying is selfishness. "Ego preachers" spend more time telling God what they want than they do in seeking to know God's will. It is one matter to tell God what we desire; it is quite another to ask God for guidance to follow His plan.

A mother overheard her young son praying. When he finished his prayer, she suggested, "Son, quit giving God orders and just report for duty." We ministers need to heed her words.

3. Be prepared everytime you go to the pulpit. I realize there are tremendous demands on a pastor's time. It is not easy to allot much time every day for sermon preparation. But time for sermon preparation is a necessity in a man's ministry, or that ministry will become a disaster.

For over thirty years in the pastorate, I experienced the same problems in finding time for sermon preparation that you as a pastor face right now. I know the pitfalls all too well: interruptions of all kinds, meetings to attend, church administration, and still more administration, a church staff to supervise, funerals and weddings, emergency calls to make dealing with all kinds of crises, multiple conferences with church members and others, seemingly insignificant misunderstandings to settle or try to solve, deadlines for bulletins and other writing assignments, financial concerns that often sap your energies, visits to the hospitals, homes, and nursing homes, talks to make at civic clubs, Sunday School classes, mission meetings, and other functions, invocations to give at different affairs in the community, and many, many other demands that space will not permit naming. If pastors are not careful, their sermon preparation will get the "leftover time"—or no time at all.

Then what is a pastor to do? Can he neglect these important areas of his ministry? No, most of the matters mentioned above must be done by the pastor, but not all of them are essential. Some items can and must be left undone. A minister must learn two lessons in dealing with many of these time-consuming matters. First, he must learn where his priorities are. He must ask, "What are the most important things I should and must do?" Second, learn how to delegate responsibility. Where does this place sermon preparation? It places it right at the top of your ministry. If you do not have time to prepare to preach, you are too busy. Drop some things, and put this matter of preparation where it belongs— at the top. If you do not have time to prepare, "make time."

Will every Sunday sermon be graded A+? No, it does not mean every sermon will be tip-top. Even "home run hitters" strike out often. But just as there is no excuse for going to bat without practice, it is also inexcusable to preach without preparation. What may seem like a poor sermon to the preacher on any given Sunday may be a tremendous spiritual blessing to someone who needs that particular message. We must never underestimate the power of the Holy Spirit to take what seems weak to us and make it God's strength for someone else.

Sermon preparation is more than merely making an outline, reading some commentaries for suggestions and interpretation of the Scriptures, and then preparing a manuscript or however you arrange your sermon. Sermon preparation involves reading God's Word for enlightenment and information. It means bathing yourself in fervent prayer to God for direction and help. The reading of good books and magazines is a part of sermon preparation.

One facet of sermon preparation probably not known by the average layperson, and often neglected even by many ministers, is a term quoted by Dr. Harold T. Bryson, professor of preaching at New Orleans Baptist Theological Seminary. Bryson referred to "creative brooding," which is the title of Robert Raines's book. Raines means for us to do some thinking on our own about a passage or character in the Bible without using somebody else's outline or sermon. Brood over the text for quite a while before reading what some· well-known pastor or teacher has written about it.

I have made a practice for years of "thinking through" the passage and making my own skeleton outline before reading what William Barclay or Alexander Maclaren and others wrote about a certain passage or Bible character. I do this because there is such temptation to feel that what Barclay and others have to say would be better than ours. But if we meditate on a passage and brood over it long enough, we can come up with thoughts we can feel good about using as the basic outline for our sermons.

Pastors need more time for creative brooding—a time when the body slows down to let the mind think and to ask the Holy Spirit in that quiet time to guide them into fields of spiritual refreshment.

4. Preach every sermon as a "dying man to dying men," not to impress a certain crowd but to glorify a great God and magnify His Son Jesus. (1) People are not interested in hearing "How Great I Am" but "How Great Thou Art." If a preacher must brag, brag on Jesus. (2) Most of the people who attend worship hour come to hear "what God says," not to be impressed with man's greatness or accomplishments.

A certain pastor wanted to help one of his friends find another pastorate. He contacted a pastorless church about his friend and made all the arrangements for the friend to preach in his own church pulpit on a specific Sunday. His friend made the journey from another state and preached in the host pastor's pulpit for the pastor search committee to meet him and hear him. The host pastor listened to his friend's sermon along with the rest of the congregation. But as the sermon progressed, the friend said less and less about Jesus Christ's redeeming love, or even how to mature in the Christian faith, and more and more about his own human accomplishments. The change of thought was obvious to the host pastor; he felt it must have been true with the pastor search committee too. The pastor graciously turned his study room over to the pastor search committee and visiting preacher after the worship hour for a private conference together. But that was the last meeting between the visiting minister and the visiting committee. Without being judgmental, it was evident that somewhere along the sermon trail the visiting speaker left the main path of God's Word and wandered off into a self-made "ego trip," never to return for the rest of the sermonic journey.

One cannot say for sure that the committee was "turned off" when he "turned self on," but since the committee parted—never to return as one of his hearers—it would indicate that something certainly went wrong. The best answer would be: "But the Holy Spirit was not in that man going to that church." Yes, that sounds like a simplistic solution to the failure of the committee to pursue their interest in that man. But remember, the Holy Spirit always magnifies Jesus Christ. Why should He expect anything less from His "called ones."

5. Use discretion in preaching every message, but never compromise your convictions about God's Word or change the content of your sermon to please a pastor search committee to gain "spiritual points."

On one occasion in one of my pastorates, I learned on Sunday afternoon that I was to have a pastor search committee in our worship hour that evening. My sermon was already prepared. As a part of that message I had already planned to read a quote from a book which I rarely, if ever, do. The words were from a minister of another denomination. In fact, he was of another race, and I mentioned his racial background. Knowing where the church was located, I knew the moment I mentioned his name and race that the committee would be "turned off" by his potent remarks of truth. Quick as a flash, it crossed my mind that if I really wanted to be heard and considered by that committee I needed to leave that quote out of my message. But the Holy Spirit had led me to include that in my "prepared sermon." Leaving it out would have been cowardice.

The flashing thought left my mind as quickly as it had gained entrance. I gave the quote, the man's name, and his race. I personally believe that contributed to their immediate exit at the close of the worship hour, and I never did hear from them again. I am not brazen enough to think that the above committee would have called me under any circumstances (maybe God used that very incident to keep me where I was). But I am saying it did not enhance my chances of being heard the second time by that committee. However, one fact became certain out of that experience: I did not lose the interest and respect of the One whose message I had prepared and delivered. Had I changed my thoughts in that sermon I might have had my ears tickled with commendations, but I would have felt God's condemnation. I felt good spiritually to avoid the latter. Besides, had that church called me I would not be writing these words to my fellow pastors. That committee's decision was one of the temporary disappointments in my life. Following the leadership of the Holy Spirit leaves a mark of joy in the heart that is a permanent memory.

   6. Work in your pastorate or other Christian church-related endeavor day by day as if you plan to spend the rest of your life in that place. However, desire the Lord's will enough that your ears and heart will be open so you will follow His leadership if He should want you to go some other place the next day.

   In one of my pastorates, our church had Dr. Marshall Craig from Dallas, Texas, as our revival leader. I remember so well what he said one day: "No church is looking for a pastor who is not working hard in his present pastorate and is always wanting to leave." From a human standpoint, there are times when we all feel like we would like to move to another place. My boyhood pastor, Dr. J. Dean Crain, said something I have never forgotten. "Early in my own ministry I used to resign every Monday morning." I did not really understand what he meant then, but over thirty-eight years in the ministry have educated me about this statement.

   Many pastors want to move every time a crisis takes place in their ministry. Still others seem to have "itchy feet" and do not stay long at any one place. But regardless of the human element of wanting to move, such a mood should never diminish a pastor's desire to work because "the night cometh, when no man can work" (John 9:4).

7. Keep loving your people. The Christian's badge of identity with Christ is found in 1 John 3:14: "We know that we have passed from death unto life, because we love the brethren." This includes the pastor, even though he encounters some church members who are uncooperative and works with others who are critical of most people in general and the pastor in particular.

The church people know whether they are just tolerated by their pastor or really loved by him. Most of the time when people are "tolerated," they are manipulated for personal gain. But when genuine love is the core of a man's ministry to his people, they will feel that love expressed toward them. Even if some do not respond to that love, they at least know it is available when and if they change.

I seriously doubt if a pastor can have an effective ministry without loving his people. One may preach good sermons, visit the sick, perform the administrative duties, and promote the church program. But if he does not love his people, they will know it.

Pastors who love only those who love them will soon discover that they have a very limited ministry. Jesus clearly taught that exclusiveness has no place in the Kingdom work. His strongest denunciations were against the extremely religious leaders of His day who refused to love those who did not fit into their little exclusive circle. But His greatest love was expressed to those outside such a circle: the sinners, the publicans, the misfortunate, and a host of others who needed compassion demonstrated.

A pastor's genuine love for people qualifies him to preach a gospel that comforts the afflicted and afflicts the comfortable. Without that kind of love for people, a pastor will be more easily misunderstood and often misinterpreted.

Pastor, keep loving your people. You are their leader, and they look to you for guidance and help. And that love has a way of revealing itself even to visitors in the worship hours.

2
Getting a Pastor Search Committee to Visit and/or Hear You Preach

Recently, a pastor said wittily, "I'm disgusted and provoked at those pulpit committees." "Why?" asked another pastor. "Because they don't come to see me," was his quick comeback. Perhaps many pastors feel this way, and they are not joking. For denominations with an autonomous form of church government, without a bishop or superintendent to appoint or assign pastors to various churches, there has to be some method of placing pastors' names before churches looking for pastors.

Let me reemphasize without any hesitation that the Holy Spirit is the Person who will be the guide and advocate in leading and bringing a pastorless congregation and undershepherd together. But I repeat, God does use human instruments.

Before we look at what sources or instruments the Holy Spirit uses, the question must be asked of every individual who wants to get his name before a church: Why do you want your name before a pastor search committee? And the "why" ought to be answered by asking another question: Are you qualified to be pastor of a church? I am not referring to one's ability. Neither am I making reference to being licensed to preach or ordained to the gospel ministry.

I personally believe there are at least three qualifications one must have to become pastor of any church.

● First, foremost, and primarily essential for one to be pastor of a church is an absolute and unequivocable call of God. The Holy Spirit must be the one agent who determines a person's call to the ministry.

A person is not called to the ministry by Uncle Joe or Aunt Susie, nor even by a praying mother "who wants her child in the ministry." People do *not* call people to the ministry.

A dedicated and seasoned pastor may have perfectly good intentions when he speaks of the large number of "preacher boys" who have come from his church, but if any of them are not "God's preacher boys," they would do well to find another place of service.

One ought to be positive about the call of God before he spends so many months and years of preparation for the gospel ministry, only to find out after a year or two—or perhaps much longer—that the enchantment of the pulpit and pews cannot be equated with the call of God to a field of service that is glorious and rewarding indeed—but at the same time quite frustrating and demanding. If God's call is not present in one's pastorate, he is in for a rude and bewildering awakening.

● Second, another qualification for pastoring a church is an endowment of gifts. I firmly believe that when God calls a person to preach and pastor a church, He endows that individual with enough gifts of the Spirit (1 Cor. 12 and Rom. 12) to do what God calls him to do.

Does God really call a person to preach His Word and pastor His "flock" without giving that individual the gift to preach and to be an undershepherd?

Some of our greatest preachers and pastors have overcome many seemingly insurmountable obstacles, such as speech impediments, timidity, or fear of standing before people. Others have been used of the Lord mightily in spite of daily dealing with severe physical handicaps. But with the positive assurance that God called them and with "fire" in their bones like Jeremiah experienced, they have turned their handicaps into blessings.

I sincerely believe that the call of God, plus the endowment of gifts necessary for preaching and pastoring a church, will put individuals in a place where God can use them.

● Third, all ministers who know they are called of God and are endowed with the gifts of the Spirit to pastor a church ought to have another important qualification, and that is preparation for the gospel ministry. I believe that commensurate with the call to preach is the call to prepare to preach and pastor. A God-called minister will "Study to shew thyself [himself] approved unto God" (2 Tim. 2:15).

I did not say a minister must have a college or seminary degree in order to pastor a church. Many pastors have had remarkable pastorates without the privilege of securing a formal education or earning a degree. However, those who do have the privilege of obtaining an education ought to take advantage of the opportunity.

Furthermore, if a minister is called to a church and wants to stay there, he must continue to prepare for ministry. The pastor who continually "gives out the Word" every week without "taking in" will soon be "on the way out" of that local church. If a pastor is to "stay qualified" for the pastorate, he must continually study the Word, read good books, and other materials in preparation for his messages and take advantage of attending as many good conferences and seminars related to his work as possible.

Now, what sources or instruments does the Holy Spirit use to get names of ministers to pastor search committees and churches? Let us look at a few.

1. Prayer.—Make it a matter of daily prayer for God to open up a new place of service. God wants His children to ask and keep on asking. He knows when a pastor needs to move, of course, but He still honors those who approach His throne with boldness and make known their requests. And it is good to remember that just as God does not "pay off on Saturday" neither does He move a pastor everytime the pastor wants to move. His timetable is quite different from our own.

The greatest source of help any minister can secure is to ask the Holy Spirit's aid in times of need concerning a place of ministry. Even when people try to hinder the advancement of His cause in a local church, prayer does wonders to lengthen and strengthen a pastor's ministry. And when God wants a pastor to change pastorates, He does listen and guide. We must be so careful in our praying about a move that we do not confuse God's will with our human desires.

2. The Resumé.—(I will go more into detail on this subject because so many have never prepared a resumé). Resumé, the French word for *summary*, is what Bob Dale calls "your ministry history in *Reader's Digest* condensed style."[1]

Also, this written summary of one's history is called a biographical sketch or vita. A resumé ought to tell a pastor search committee about the minister's qualifications and abilities in ministry. How one looks on paper may be the one source to lead a committee to hear or interview a minister. In fact, Dr. Dale says, "Your resumé serves only one purpose—to create a good first impression.[2]

A resumé will *not* get a minister a church or change of pastorates. A combination of factors converge in the call of a pastor to a church—the Holy Spirit being the leading person. But the resumé can give a minister a contact with a church. Prospective pastors need to realize that most pastor search committees request and insist on some kind of biographical material before they hear a minister preach and certainly before a church calls a pastor.

Writing a resumé for a pastor search committee is quite different from writing one for a business office. The pastor and church ought to be businesslike, but the church is not a business. It is an eleemosynary institution—a nonprofit fellowship even if the church is incorporated for legal purposes. For example, a business executive or personnel office of a large firm might not want a picture attached to a resumé. But personally I have found that the pastor search committees using a state convention office of church-ministers relations want pictures of prospective pastors. Also, I have observed that committees want smiling and pleasant-looking pictures of pastors. The pictures should be billfold size in black and white for copying purposes.

In addition to the above, I have observed too that members of these committees want information about a pastor's financial compensation and how he feels about the mission program of his denomination. If you use the services of one of the state convention offices, you may be asked to complete one of their standard resumé forms. It would be to your advantage to do so.

Such a form may look similar to the one on pages 27-29. A recap of the form then follows on pages 30-31.

DATE _____

BIOGRAPHICAL INFORMATION

**USE THIS SPACE
FOR A CURRENT
WALLET-SIZED
PHOTOGRAPH
(Black & White)**

Please type if possible. Only the first part of this form will be used for press release, denominational programs, or other public relations projects. The rest of the material, beginning with the references, will be CONFIDENTIAL and will be copied for authorized pastor search committees only.

NAME _____

HOME ADDRESS _____
                        (Street)

_____
(City)   (State)   (Zip)

TELEPHONE (R) _____(W) _____AGE _____MARITAL STATUS _____

BIRTHDATE _____BIRTHPLACE _____WIFE'S MAIDEN NAME _____
                                                        (OR HUSBAND'S NAME)

WIFE'S HOME TOWN _____CHILDREN'S AGES _____CHILDREN AT HOME _____

FORMAL EDUCATION:

HIGH SCHOOL _____YEAR GRADUATED _____

COLLEGE_____YEAR_____DEGREE_____

SEMINARY _____YEAR _____DEGREE _____

OTHER _____

LICENSED? _____YEAR _____BY WHAT CHURCH _____STATE _____

ORDAINED? _____YEAR _____BY WHAT CHURCH _____STATE _____

EXPERIENCE:

YEARS	CHURCH OR ORGANIZATION	LOCATION	SIZE	POSITION
____to____				
____to____				
____to____				
____to____				
____to____				
____to____				
____to____				

PRESENT EMPLOYMENT _____

If Bi-Vocational (jointly with church employment): Company _____Telephone # _____

Work as a _____Hours per week _____

DENOMINATIONAL SERVICE: (Include major positions held. writings. teaching assignments for assemblies. retreats. etc)

CIVIC/COMMUNITY ACTIVITIES:

BUSINESS AND/OR MILITARY EXPERIENCE:

HOBBIES OR OTHER SPECIAL INTEREST ABILITIES: (Music. drama. etc)

OTHER:

CONFIDENTIAL REFERENCES:

CHURCH RELATED:

1 _____ ADDRESS _____

2 _____ ADDRESS _____

OTHER THAN CHURCH RELATED:

1 _____ ADDRESS _____

2 _____ ADDRESS _____

INFORMATION ON YOUR PRESENT CHURCH/ORGANIZATION

Downtown _____ City _____ Suburban _____ Small City _____ Town _____ Rural _____

College _____ Resident membership _____ Budget, year 19 _____ $ _____

OTHER STAFF _____

PRESENT COMPENSATION SUMMARY:
1. Salary and Housing
   Base Salary . . . . Amount . . . . _____
   Housing:
      Pastorium _____ . . . . Fair Market Value . . . . _____
      or
      Housing Allowance _____ . . . . _____
   Utilities Allowance . . . . _____
                                           Total Salary $ _____

2. Protection Benefits
   Retirement percentage: _____ . . . . _____
   Group Life Insurance . . . . _____
   Long Term Disability Insurance . . . . _____
   Medical-Hospitalization . . . . _____
   Other, such as Social Security . . . . _____
      (Note: Ordained ministers considered self-employed)
                            Total Protection Benefits $ _____

3. Service Ministries (NON-SALARY)
   Car Expenses . . . . _____
   Convention Expenses . . . . _____
   Books and Continuing Education . . . . _____
   Other _____ _____
                       Total Service Ministries $ _____

FAMILY DATA:

Wife's (or Husband) education _____

How does your wife (or Husband) feel about your ministry _____

_____

HOW DO YOU FEEL ABOUT AND SUPPORT THE MISSION PROGRAM OF YOUR DENOMINATION? _____

_____

_____

CHANGE: Check your present attitude toward making a change
☐ a. I am interested in making a change
☐ b. I would consider a change . . .
☐ c. I would not consider a change now.
   If you were to consider moving, please check the position or positions in which you would be interested:
☐ Pastor   ☐ Minister of Education   ☐ Minister of Youth   ☐ Associate Pastor   ☐ Minister of Music
☐ Minister of Evangelism and Outreach   ☐ Other_____

PERMISSION IS HEREBY GIVEN TO DUPLICATE THE ABOVE DATE FOR THE USE OF PASTOR-SEARCH (PULPIT COMMITTEES) OR PERSONNEL COMMITTEES:

                        SIGNATURE _____

● It identifies you immediately and gives the basic personal information a committee will want to know about you. Our office has received a few resumés where the reader actually had to "hunt" the person's name and address. Pastor search committees do not and will not spend time "hunting for information" when they have so many other resumés in hand.

● Next, it gives room for concise information about a minister's educational background.

● The space given to church or organizational experience is extremely important. You can begin with your most recent place of ministry and trace your work back to your earliest responsibility in ministry.

● The form then gives the minister an opportunity to list some marks of professional leadership in denominational service and secular work, including writings and civic activities. There is room to name some of the gifts of the Spirit you have used in your ministry. Pastor search committees are eager to know how God has used your life in the past and what you can do for Him through their local church and community in the future.

● Of course there is space for you to list some references. Often we get resumés with ten or fifteen references, which is far, far too many. Be sure you have permission from the individuals to use their names as references.

● If you are a student or do not now pastor a church, it is not necessary to fill in the section dealing with compensation.

● Since missions and evangelism ought to be of vital importance in any church of any denomination you are encouraged to include that in your resumé. Many churches will not call a pastor who will not support a strong missions program.

If you do not want to use the services of a denominational church-ministers relations office, make your own form but make it orderly. Center your name at the top of the first page in capital letters and include the following in your resumé:

(1) Your current address and telephone number on the top left margin with your birthdate and marital and family status on the top right side of the page.

(2) State your ministry goal: "pastor."

(3) List separately your experience in the ministry according to places and time, beginning with your latest place of service.

(4) Trace your educational background, listing degrees and years of graduation.

(5) Then list denominational places of service, including writings, conferences led at assemblies, and other leadership roles.

(6) Note your gifts for ministry and how God has given you opportunities to use them.

(7) And give a few references of people who know you and your past work.

Should you think it best not to include a photograph or other information about yourself, leave it out. Be your judge along this line.

Regardless of what resumé form you follow, please keep certain vital matters in mind as you prepare and write the material:

• Typing it is much better than writing. If you cannot type, ask a trusted friend to do it for you, even if you have to pay to have it done. Use a good grade of paper that can be used several times if copies are made from it.

• Be neat. A messy resumé speaks louder than you may realize. Neatness speaks volumes about a person's habits and character.

• Use good English and correct spelling, even though you do not need to use full sentences.

• Make it brief. Long resumés are simply not read. Our office received one recently that was fifteen pages long. Your resumé should be brief enough to give the committee a "bird's-eye picture" of you and your ministry but long enough to reveal a true story of your family, education, and especially your experience in ministry. One to three pages is certainly enough.

Please accept the fact that more and more pastor search committees are requesting resumés. This may be one of the most valuable instruments and sources the Holy Spirit wants to use to place your name before a committee. If you are reluctant to use a resumé because you have limited education and/or experience, let me assure you that God can read too. He does not limit His work by using only the most educated and experienced ministers. This does not mean God frowns on education and experience, however.

3. Pastors. Pastors recommending pastors to pastorless churches is probably one of the most frequently used sources of placing prospective pastors' names before pastor search committees.

I have known a number of dedicated pastors who are quite reluctant about asking anyone to give their names to churches seeking pastors, even when they feel a change is needed. It is not unethical to ask a fellow pastor to share your name. However, it is understandable why a few pastors feel like they do about asking pastors to give their names to churches without pastors. Many pastors may have a tendency to "overintroduce" or exaggerate the gifts or talents of their pastor friends.

● Make it clear that you would want him to give your name only to churches where he feels led by the Holy Spirit.

● Never ask several pastors to write letters of recommendation about you to the same church. Committees become suspicious of an individual pastor when they receive "campaign letters," and they have reason to feel there is collusion. Campaigning for a church hurts every "God-called man" and lowers the dignity of the office.

Some pastors share pastor friends' names with churches without being asked to do so. God does work through pastors to help other pastors.

4. Directors of Missions.—Some denominations are divided into districts or associations with a leader or director over each district. These directors are closely associated with the churches and know when vacancies occur. They are key people to know and contact.

When you do give your resumé to one of these directors, keep these matters in mind:

● There is usually a limit as to how long a director will keep your file active. So keep in touch.

● Write a personal letter to the director, along with your resumé, not a mimeographed sheet you will send to a dozen other people.

● If you need to talk with the director in person, make an appointment before you make the visit.

● When you move, contact the director immediately so he will not continue to share your name with churches. If you change addresses but do not find a church, please contact him and give him your new address.

It certainly helps to be active in your association or district long before you need to move.

5. *Church-Ministers Relations Offices of the Various State Conventions.*—I know from firsthand experience that the directors of these departments want to help the pastors and churches. They provide biographical information on ministers to the churches without recommendation, interpretation, or evaluation. Materials concerning the work of the pastor search committees are furnished upon request. Also, personal conferences are scheduled with churches and ministers upon request.

Most of the directors of such offices visit the various seminaries in their denomination annually to interview the students from their state or district. The resumés they receive are then shared with pastorless churches.

In light of the above information, *what can these directors do to help a pastor or theological school graduate get a pastor search committee to visit and/or hear him preach?*

● Make it possible for any minister to file biographical information (resumé) with the office.

● Share this information with inquiring churches who are without pastors.

● Counsel with any pastor who feels that he needs to move and assure him that his resumé will be shared with various pastorless churches.

● Listen when a minister hurts and be that minister's friend. I believe all of the church-ministers relations directors have served as pastors and have empathy toward other undershepherds.

● Be fair to everybody.

● Encourage the pastor search committees to thoroughly investigate a minister before calling him.

What can a pastor or theological seminary graduate or Bible school graduate do to help his denomination's Church-Ministers Relations Office help the pastors and graduates?

● Keep in touch with the church-ministers relations office in your state. If you are wanting to move, let the director know it.

Let the office know at least once a month that you want your name to remain in the active file. If you have a change of address, notify the office immediately.

• Keep your resumé up-to-date and make it factual.

• If you contact the state director by mail, write a personal letter—*not* one that is mimeographed and sent to "several others."

• Please be patient with the office. After your name is shared, it is up to the church or churches to contact you, not the office. Where the resumés are sent is kept confidential.

• If you do not wish for the department to continue to share your name, please contact the office and ask that your file be "deactivated."

• If you should move to another church, please let the office know so your name will not be mailed out to churches looking for a pastor.

6. Schools.—Most of the schools and seminaries will try to help their graduates find placement in churches after graduation. Pastors should feel free to write them when they need help.

7. State Convention Offices.—Since all state conventions in various denominations do not have church-ministers relations departments, feel free to contact the offices of the various state conventions and let them know of your availability.

8. Friends and Former Church Members.—Contacts can be made through various friends and former church members who would feel free to share your name with other churches.

Before closing this section I want to answer a question that is often asked, "How do some pastors get their names before so many pastor search committees, and others rarely, if ever, have any contact with such committees?" There are many answers to this question.

From a positive standpoint, it must be stated that:

• Many pastors have unusual amounts of charisma, and people are naturally drawn to hear them.

• Other pastors have multiple gifts of the Spirit and they are mightily used of the Lord.

• Still other pastors have greater abilities than average, and churches hear about their work. Such abilities, along with the right spirit, enhance their likelihood of being considered by several challenging churches.

● Some pastors may not have the above characteristics, but for some reason only God knows, the Holy Spirit lays His hand on them and blesses them with unusual opportunities and tremendous usefulness.

●And truthfully it must be noted that many pastors who have opportunities to be heard by several pastor search committees happen to be in the right places at the right times.

From a negative standpoint, I must add that other sources, which are abhorred by other ministers, are used by some ministers.

● Some pastors have an uncanny method of "pushing themselves." They seem to know when and where almost every pulpit is vacant.

I once knew a pastor whose main topic of conversation was: "I know five good churches that are open right now." Then he proceeded to name the churches. He read all the state papers and marked down what churches were vacant and where they were located. He then proceeded to contact "the network" of friends who would make his contacts.

Letter writing is one practice that follows inquiry about vacant pulpits. Some ministers contact several of their minister friends and launch a letter-writing campaign to a pastor search committee of a certain church. Others select some outstanding and well-known leader among pastors to write such a letter. Others write their own letters of recommendation to certain pulpit committees.

● One pastor search committee member discovered that a pastor called by telephone and recommended that a friend of his ought to be considered by the committee. The "friend" happened to be himself, even though he kept saying, "He will make you an excellent pastor."

● A few pastors actually call pastor search committees on the telephone and make it plain: "I want to get my name before your committee." Pastor search committee chairmen have told me of several pastors doing this.

● Needless to note, other methods and sources can be used by ministers to "pick a good plum," but such registers a negative feeling to the majority of pastors.

Many pastor search committees are wise enough to know the difference between the ministers seeking to "land" certain churches and those being sought. Other committees fail to see or catch the difference. Let me declare emphatically that unscrupulous means may be used to secure the pulpit of a certain church, but nine times out of ten such methods will not help a pastor keep that church. Unethical practices never enhance a person's ministry; they only compound the troubles.

It is far better for one to miss a certain church and still keep integrity than it is to get a certain church and not be able to live with oneself, or the congregation.

I repeat as a summary: the Holy Spirit is the One who can send a pastor search committee to visit and/or hear any pastor. He is not limited by a pastor's desire to stay in a particular church or by another undershepherd's eagerness to move. The Spirit's aid and guidance ought to be the final authority.

At the same time, two definite truths should be kept in mind:

(1) A pastor may grieve the Holy Spirit by avoiding His will and following the human "hunch" or will.

(2) Also a pastor has many human instruments at his disposal for the Holy Spirit to use to get his name before a pastor search committee: a few out of a multitude have been discussed above.

3
When a Committee Contacts You

I try to encourage pastor search committees to visit a prospective pastor before they formally hear him preach. I suggest they call him by telephone, identify themselves, state their purpose, and mutually set up an agreed time (other than during the Sunday or Wednesday worship hours), so they can get acquainted with the prospective pastor. I encourage them to simply state: "We are a pastor search committee of the East Church. Your name has been given to us as a prospective pastor. Without any obligation on your part or ours, I would like for us to get together for a time of fellowship and sharing about our need of a pastor." They may want to meet at your church or home or at a specific restaurant for a meal together. The purpose of the visit is simply to learn something about each other and give the Holy Spirit an opportunity to give His guidance as to their future work.

Some pastor search committees may want the prospective pastor to visit their church for the same purpose. If this should take place, the church making this request should meet all of the prospective pastor's expenses.

While the above is more ideal, the average church will most likely want to visit the prospective pastor's church and hear him preach before anything transpires. In the written material I share with pastor search committees, and during the personal conferences I have with committees, I definitely encourage the church seeking a pastor to call the prospective pastor by telephone and ask the following questions:

1. Will you be preaching in your pulpit this Sunday?

2. Would it be convenient for our committee to visit your church and hear you preach?

3. Are you dealing with another pastor search committee at the present time?

4. May we meet with you after the worship hour?

I tell the committee that calling the pastor in advance has some real advantages:

(1) It may save a needless trip if he is not preaching that Sunday.

(2) The pastor can arrange his schedule to talk with the committee after the worship hour.

(3) If he is dealing with another pastor search committee, it would be better to say, "We appreciate your honesty. It would be wise for our committee not to visit you at the present time. If it does not work out for you to go to that church as pastor let us know. We may still want to visit your church and hear you preach."

(4) By talking with the pastor directly, the committee may receive some information they would not be able to secure from anyone else.

Again, while the above is the ideal, many committees do not follow these procedures. Some committees still like to "slip in and slip out" as if unnoticed. Even though it is almost impossible for the committee to make a secret visit, many churches still prefer this procedure so they may avoid what they call a "sugar-stick" sermon.

If a pastor search committee contacts you by telephone, here are some suggestions you may want to consider *before* the committee actually visits you or hears you preach:

1. If you are not interested in moving, at least graciously thank them for their call and state why you feel they should not make the visit at the present time.

2. If the committee insists on hearing you, even though you do not want to leave your present church, do not try to talk the committee out of visiting you. God may be in that visit, and you may not be aware of it. Give the Holy Spirit an opportunity to guide you.

3. If you have had a deluge of pastor search committees to visit

your church recently, and you feel that too many committees are disturbing your congregation or hurting your ministry, it may be best to thank the inquiring committee and simply explain that "it would be better at the present time for you not to visit our church." There are times when too many committees might give your present church the feeling you are trying to leave, and this could jeopardize your work there.

4. Still again, if you have had too many pastor search committees of late, and the committee insists on visiting you or hearing you preach, why not suggest you meet them at their church or a restaurant during a weekday and merely get acquainted. Such a conversation could or could not lead to further inquiry or a call to their church. Be sure you do not "close the door" on the leadership of the Holy Spirit.

It is easy to say, "I wish pastor search committees did things differently." Remember, it is an honor to be contacted by a pastor search committee. Since most members of these committees have had very little training or experience in this field, simply be grateful for them and remember them in your prayers.

4
When a Committee Actually Visits You and Hears You Preach

There is a tremendous difference in a pastor search committee contacting you and actually visiting you or hearing you preach. Sometimes a committee will make contact with a pastor through a church secretary and ask, "Is the pastor preaching this Sunday?" Still again, such a committee may actually talk with a pastor by phone and even indicate an interest in hearing him preach. That does not mean they will absolutely and positively make a visit.

Last-minute changes on the part of one or more members of the committee may completely alter their plans. Another new name may be given to the committee the following week, and they may never show at all. Pastors must be prepared for all kinds of changes and disappointments when pastor search committees make initial contacts.

This chapter deals with a pastor search committee really visiting and hearing a prospective minister speak. They may or may not have called by phone.

1. What should a pastor do when he knows a pastor search committee is in the worship services and will hear him preach?

(1) *Preach what you have prepared to preach.* Do not change your subject. Preach what the Holy Spirit led you to prepare.

(2) *Use the same style of preaching you usually use* or had already planned to use. Being unnatural to impress a few people may backfire instead of hitting the target. Throwing in a few extra intellectual statements for the sake of enhancing your sermon or adding a corny joke to spice up the contents may turn sour when strangers try to digest them.

(3) *Preach to the whole congregation*—not specifically to the commit-

tee. The committee may easily know whether you are preaching for them or to the congregation.

(4) *Be yourself and act as normal and natural as possible.*

2. What if the committee leaves after the worship hour and does not converse with you?

(1) The committee that does *not* speak to you after the sermon may or may not be interested in further contact with you.

a. Sometimes a committee will leave the building and discuss their future plans as they travel home or at the next regular committee meeting.

b. They may make plans to come back and hear you again, with or without advance notice.

c. Often a committee will put a pastor "on the back burner" and make a return visit after they have heard several other pastors preach.

d. The same committee may wait until they get home, and if they feel you are not "God's man" for their church at the present time, they may write you a letter saying, "We feel led to look in a different direction." That settles it, and you should not look for a return visit from them.

e. Still again, they may write you and send certain materials about their church. Most of the time when this happens, the committee will make a return visit to hear you preach and talk with you at length.

(2) Do not feel like you have been neglected if the committee leaves without speaking to you. It does not necessarily mean you "struck out" with your sermon. Even if the committee never contacts you or never returns to hear you, it still does not mean you "flunked" on that Sunday.

3. What if that committee *does* converse with you at the close of the worship hour? Does this mean they are interested in pursuing a call to you? Here again that may or may not be true:

(1) I encourage *every* committee to talk with *every* minister they hear at the close of the worship hour, whether or not they are interested in him.

(2) Also, I encourage every committee to write a letter to the

pastor they hear when they return home, whether or not they are interested in pursuing the visit.

(3) And, in all fairness to the pastor and the church, I encourage the committee to hear a prospective pastor at least twice before calling him as their pastor.

4. Please keep one idea in mind: what I have discussed above is "the ideal." I wish every pastor search committee would follow these suggestions. You and I realize that every committee does not follow these methods, even when they have information about good procedures.

So, if a committee visits you, be prepared for any number of events, usual or unusual. The most important element, regardless of procedures, is for the Holy Spirit to take charge. He is the One we want to please. If He guides you to another place of service, He will overcome any human blunders, mistakes, or detours.

5

How Should You Conduct Yourself
When a Committee Interviews You?

Let us assume that the very committee which heard you preach that sermon wants to meet you personally for an interview. Or perhaps the same committee will return to their homes without speaking to you, but will make a second visit to hear you preach and then want to meet with you personally.

How should you conduct yourself?

1. If the committee should invite you (and probably your spouse, if married) to lunch or dinner at the close of the worship hour, try your best to make arrangements to accept. If you pastor in a rural area or a small town and eat at a local restaurant, be prepared for your membership to find out you are meeting with a pastor search committee, because word will travel.

2. If you have small children and need to care for them during the meal, the committee may suggest that they come back to your home or church later that day. This happened to me during one of my pastorates when I had two small sons. The committee was wise enough to realize that my wife could not comfortably carry on a good conversation with two children to feed and watch. When they returned to our home at 2 o'clock, both my wife and I were able to sit in the living room in a relaxed fashion and talk with the committee.

3. In either of the above situations, or even at another time, certain suggestions are helpful:

• Do more listening than talking to the committee. If they are vitally interested in you, you will have plenty of time to ask questions at a later time. Take advantage of the present time to become acquainted with the committee and church. Be more concerned about establishing a relationship during this first interview.

• Express "warmth" in your conversation. Committees are looking for pastors who can communicate the love of Christ, and feelings of warmth are more indicative of that love.

• Use good "eye contact." Looking away as you talk gives an expression of insecurity and lack of confidence.

• Try to stay calm and relaxed and have good posture as you communicate with them. Do not be "overanxious." "Play it cool."

• Sincerity is always noticed by people who are looking for leaders. People want authentic ministers—not phonies.

• Do not make too many demands in your discussion about your ministry.

• Be honest with them about your strengths and weaknesses, but do not overemphasize either. Do not oversell or undersell yourself.

• Express a good image of yourself. Do not "knock" yourself. There is no use of maximizing your faults: they will find those out soon enough if you become their pastor.

• If your spouse is present in this first interview, give your spouse an opportunity to express their feelings too. A word of caution is in order: a spouse who dominates the interview will most likely be suspected by the committee as a "domineering" spouse, and this will be looked upon as a liability rather than an asset.

I have heard committees say, "We like Reverend Blow, but we have some doubts about 'the other half.' "

On the other hand, it does not help the minister one bit when he shows impatience with his spouse during the interview or calls attention to the negative aspects of his life.

• Do *not* talk negatively about the problems you face in your present church. This does not mean you are "hiding some truth," but it does mean a committee may "be turned off" when a prospective pastor talks about his own problems. A committee is not interested so much in what you *cannot* do at your present church as they are about what you *can do* in the future to help them.

● Be aware when the interview is over, and express your appreciation for their visit.

I am taking for granted that you are dressed neatly and will use proper etiquette.

Interviews are important. Simply be yourself, and ask the Lord to guide you and bless you.

6
How Can You Tell When It Is Time to Move?

One of the questions most frequently asked by pastors is: "When can I tell if it is time to move—to change churches?" Then a pastor will follow that question with statements such as these: "Well, I don't have to move, but I just feel like my work is coming to an end where I am now." Or another will say, "I've been in my present church about five years, and I just want to leave while things are going well. I don't want to stay too long and be asked to leave." Another pastor will remark, "This church never keeps a pastor over three years, and I'm approaching that time now." One pastor remarked to me, "I'd like to be the first pastor in the history of this church to leave under my own free will, without any pressure from the church."

Well, when is it time to leave a church? When things are going great and you can leave with a good spirit? Or, if things are going exceptionally well, why leave a good situation? Have pastors let congregations talk them into actually believing that any person's ministry must be limited to a certain period of time, say five years? Is that good for the pastor or the church, or both? If God calls a person to a certain church, does the same God who calls him there put a "time frame" on his ministry? Who tells a pastor that it is time to leave because the last three pastors have each left the church after three- or five-year ministries? Where does the leadership of the Holy Spirit fit into this picture, or where does the human factor enter the scene?

God and people work together. The Holy Spirit uses human agents to bring pastors and churches together. God wants our response to help accomplish His will.

First, take a look at some reasons why a pastor should not leave his present pastorate. And remember: you may be tempted to use these as excuses to move, but "in your heart" you know these are not valid reasons for leaving.

STATEMENT: "I have reached all the lost people in the community."

REPLY: This is probably not true. Even it it were true, a pastor always has a ministry to his own membership.

STATEMENT: "There are just too many problems in the church for me to solve."

REPLY: God did not call you as pastor to solve all the problems in a church. He called you to minister to the people.

STATEMENT: "The people seem so complacent and will not do anything. This seems to be a 'status quo' church. I am totally discouraged."

REPLY: This has always been true of many churches. Good leaders never give up trying to help their people.

STATEMENT: "I have taken the church as far as I can take it."

REPLY: This is probably not true. A church can always improve internally if not externally.

STATEMENT: "I know that some or many of the people want me to leave."

REPLY: Of course, some people want the pastor to leave. You will always find this true. You cannot base your call to a church on the basis of who wants you to leave.

STATEMENT: "I was misled by the pastor search committee. Things were pictured entirely different from what they really are."

REPLY: This statement can be repeated by many pastors. Many committees just do not have the expertise to give a good "overall picture" of their church. In their excitement and hope for a pastor, they often promise things to the prospective pastor that the church cannot deliver. Make the best of a bad situation until you can correct it or until you are positive God is leading you in a different direction.

STATEMENT: "I cannot get along with my staff. I inherited a bad situation." Or, "I got the wrong staff person(s)."

REPLY: This is certainly understandable. Staff problems are legion among church ministers. Sometimes they are imaginary; often they are overexaggerated; many, many times they are so real that life becomes almost unbearable. There are no easy answers about how to solve some of the above problems. Sometimes there must be a "parting of the ways" between staff personnel, and this brings anguish, hurt, and division. It is never easy to solve such problems. If a staff member refuses to cooperate with a pastor, or determines he or she will not do the assigned work outlined by the job description, drastic measures must be taken, and this is painful.

When it looks like all parties will remain "intact," they ought to sit down together and reach a reasonable decision regarding their attitude and specific duties so the church will go forward in the Spirit of Christ.

STATEMENT: "The grass looks greener on the other side. I just need a different church, different scenery."

REPLY: The grass almost always looks good from a distance. Sometimes it pays for pastors to get away from their church fields for a while and really think about their pastorates. What looks like a chore or an impossibility with everyday familiarity can become a genuine challenge.

Sometimes a pastor will remark, "Oh, if I just had a different church or a larger staff I could get so much more done, or my load would be easier." I once thought the same thing. In my first pastorate out of the seminary, a fellow pastor came by my study one morning and said, "You've got the best setup now you'll probably ever have. You have time to study, and you do not have to supervise a staff." I listened to him, but I didn't believe what he said. As my responsibilities became so much heavier in other churches, and I did the extra job of finding, supervising, and keeping a staff I learned through experience that my older fellow pastor had traveled that route long enough to know the truth of his advice. Many times after his statement I longed for those "all-morning study hours" without even a phone to disturb me. God had me in the right place at the right time. Maybe this is true of you right now, and you just don't realize it. Fertilize your grass, and it will become far greener right where you are.

STATEMENT: "I have had several pastor search committees visit our church· just recently. Is God trying to tell me something?"

REPLY: Just thank God that you have had committees to hear you. That does *not* necessarily mean you ought to move.

I recall that a pastor search committee came to hear me when I was pastor of First Baptist Church in Taylors, South Carolina. The members of that committee asked me at least to visit their church building and see their community. I remember distinctly how the committee showed me the church auditorium and then asked me to kneel with them around the pulpit. The chairman said, "Lord, we believe this young man is the pastor you want for our church. We believe we have found God's man." However, I did not feel like that at all. I knew I was not God's man for that church because I was God's man for First Baptist Church at Taylors, and I could not serve both churches.

During the last three years of my latest pastorate, I had five pastor search committees to talk with me personally about their churches. But for some reason I simply did not feel led to go beyond "the talking stage." Then when the committees left, and I went back to the everyday routine of my pastoral work, I would say to my Marilyn at later times, "Honey, why in the world didn't I at least consider visiting that church? What in the world is wrong with me?" Her answer was always the same: "Darling, God is saving you for something else. I don't know what it is, but God is saving you for another place." I must admit her faith strengthened me more than mine. She was right. God did have other plans for me. That is why I am writing this material.

Second, let us take a look at some factors and signs that may point a pastor to seriously consider moving, or changing churches.

1. *Be honest enough to ask the question: "How are my own vital signs?"*
- How is your spiritual temperature?
- What about your heart? Is it still warm for the unsaved? Do you still have a burdened heart for your people? A pastor called our office recently and reported, "I really need to move." Then he

sighed, "Brother Harbin, I've lost my burden." I knew what he meant.

● What about your breathing? Are you relying on your own power to keep you spiritually alive instead of the fresh, daily breath of God's Holy Spirit?

● Check your thinking process. Have your brain cells become so weak because of lethargy that you do not possess enough power to prepare fresh sermons week by week? Are you serving your people "warmed-over" mental and spiritual food?

● Has your spiritual, mental, and physical energy level become so low that you dread going into the pulpit to "preach God's Word"? Or do you still become excited about preaching to your people week by week?

● Does your "pulse beat" increase or decrease when you have opportunity to speak a good word about God's love to your people?

● What about your resilience? When you have a bad week, do you bounce back easily, or does it take its toll on your nervous system, and you are days and days returning to normal?

Let me ask six questions about further personal signs.

● What gives you the biggest thrill—to minister to people or to be ministered unto? It is only normal to expect some response from your ministry. But when more satisfaction is felt by ministers when they continually receive for self instead of giving to others, they have reached a low point in their pastorates.

● What about discouragement and depression? If a minister has these occasionally it is perfectly normal. Short-term depression is probably experienced by every minister. We all feel like Elijah at times—that we are the only ones suffering. If pastors have long-term periods of discouragement and depression and they rarely, if ever, find any relief from these "low experiences," something is dreadfully wrong in their pastorates. "Weeping" does take place in the night, but where is the "joy" in the morning? (Ps. 30:5).

● How is your attitude?

Have you kept a positive attitude about your daily responsibilities, or does every facet of your work seem to fall into categories of negativism?

● What effect has this had on your family and on your own health?

● Does your work irritate you? If it does, instead of challenging you to improve the quality of it, your attitude has plunged below the normal level, and you are walking on "thin ice."

● Do you feel you have lost your effectiveness? It is not unusual for some church members to think that their pastor has lost his effectiveness; the tragic problem arises when the pastor himself knows and feels that he has lost his effectiveness. Has this happened to you? If you are positive this has happened to you, what can you do about it? If you are not willing at least to "try" to improve it or correct it, you could be in the wrong place.

2. *Next, what about your membership's vital signs?* Do you have a spiritually healthy church?

A "healthy church" is a more loving and understanding church. The members are more tolerant toward each other as well as toward the pastor. When crises develop in the membership, the church as a whole has more power to sustain one another and to support the pastor.

(1) Do you sense and feel a spiritual "coldness" among the majority of your church members? It is only natural to have a small percentage of "nominal church members," but if the majority of the members have a "below-normal spiritual temperature," and the pastor cannot raise it, the church could need either new leadership or a new and fresh spiritual approach by the present pastor. If the church has been this way for many years (even before you became pastor of the church), the people may be satisfied to remain in this state of spiritual apathy and indifference. But if such a condition does not bother you and burden you, there is little likelihood that you will do anything about it.

(2) Does the church have at least a few warmhearted members who have a deep compassion for the unsaved people in the community and try to win them to the Lord?

(3) Do your people get more enjoyment out of controversy than they do out of expressing love for one another? Church people who argue and fuss with one another instead of demonstrating love for one another have heart problems.

(4) Do the worship hours in your church seem cold and mechanical rather than "Spirit-filled"? Do visitors who come to your church say, "That's the coldest church I've ever seen?" If this is true, is it a reflection on the condition of the church members or the pastor? Can you help change this feeling?

(5) When did the church experience a genuine revival? And how long did it last? If the people as a whole seem lethargic and apathetic, and the spiritual energy level is dreadfully low, the sickness needs an immediate injection of God's spiritual adrenalin.

(6) Have the people lost the desire to visit new people moving into the community, knowing that the church is in a "growing area"?

If the church has weak and tepid vital signs for a short period of time, the pastor has a good chance of helping bring about a spiritual recovery. If such a condition exists over an extremely long period of time and the pastor cannot seem to revive the "patient," in spite of years of trying and a sufficient amount of God's changing love and power, then a move might be in the best interest of both the pastor and the church.

3. *Opposition is another area that may have an influence on a pastor's decision regarding tenure at a local church.* What do pastors do if they have severe opposition, and they feel like they are facing a losing cause?

• First, make a good analysis of your opposition. Is it really as strong as you imagine it is? Many times a pastor will think he has terrific opposition and just cannot stay on as pastor. When he actually finds out how many people are against him he is amazed to discover that the opposition is not nearly as strong as he thought. Usually the opposition is composed of only a few souls, and it is not as strong as it is loud. Be sure you know the strength of your opposition before you run in fear.

• Next, consider your opposition in proportion to the size of your church. If your church is fairly large and you have several members vehemently against your ministry, they may be absorbed in the big membership. If your membership is small and you have "prominent families" or "several members" who violently oppose your ministry and refuse to cooperate in any way, you could be fighting a losing battle, especially if several people who are kinfolks have built up a power structure over the years. It would not be wise to abandon the ship because of such troubled waters, but it would be using good judgment to make it known to pastor friends and others that you might be interested in making a move. A pastor should be in daily contact with the Holy Spirit regarding the above matters. I will have more to say about the above situation in the section of the book dealing with conflict, resignation, and alternatives to resignation.

4. *Please look at one other matter concerning moving to another church or staying where you are.* Suppose you are contacted by a church. The pastor search committee has already heard you preach and want you to preach in their church in view of a call. What if you are happy where you now pastor and you do not want to leave? Or suppose you would leave if greatly challenged?

If I had it to do over again, I would at least give some thought to a challenging situation (I did not say large church) if a pastor search committee contacted me and wanted me to consider their church. I would at least visit their church building and church field.

Let me give an example. A pastor search committee came to hear me preach when I was at my last church. They had a long talk with my wife and me at a restaurant in a nearby city following the morning worship. Everything was positive in their conversation. Before we all left, the chairman said, "Now, we are obligated to hear some other prospective pastors in the next few weeks, but we will get back in touch with you." About five weeks later, I received a call from the chairman of that committee. He said, "We are still interested in you, and we want to know if you would be interested in us: yes or no?" When he said yes or no, I felt that I could not give an honest answer to that question. So I said, "Well, if I have to give an answer by phone I guess I would have to say no." When I said no, that was the last time I heard from them.

Now, I have no regrets about the answer I gave. But if I had it to do over again, I would have replied, "Jim, I just cannot give you an answer. Why not let my wife and me come to your church building and meet with your committee again? Then show us around the city and let us find out more about the area. Then if the Holy Spirit leads you to ask me to preach in your church, and if I feel the same leading, I will be most happy to do so. But as it was, I closed the door. I did not give the committee, the Holy Spirit, or myself the chance to see what would happen.

If you are interviewed or asked by a pastor search committee to visit a pastorless church or to preach for them in view of a call, I, personally, would at least: pray about it with deep earnestness; visit the church building and location; talk with the committee again and perhaps some key leaders of the church; and before I would preach in view of a call, I would want to feel about 98 percent that God was at that point leading me to that church.

What are some other criteria for a pastor to follow when a church wants to present him to their congregation for a call or actually votes to call him? I believe the following are valid reasons to guide a pastor in his decision to leave his present church if considered or called by another church:

● I have really prayed about this matter, and I believe God is in the move. It is not based on my emotions or temporary moods.

● I have enough information about the prospective church, and I believe I can be the kind of pastor they need.

● The committee has made every possible effort to be fair to me about the present and future challenges of the church.

● My decision has not been based on my personal desire to stay or leave where I am now. I have used good judgment and common sense as I have thought and prayed through this matter.

● I feel that I would be going against the will of God if I do not accept this new challenge.

● I have discussed this call with my spouse and family, and they are reconciled that I believe God is leading me to a new field of service. This does not mean everybody in the family must be happy about the situation.

● I have sought advice and prayer from a "trusted friend" of mine. We have prayed together about the situation.

It is never easy to seek and find the will of God. When a pastor leaves one church for another place of service and knows God is in the move, it ushers a genuine peace into the heart.

7

What Should a Pastor Tell the Present Congregation or Deacons When He Preaches at Another Church in View of a Call?

I realize this is an individual matter. Some pastors tell the deacons in a regular or called deacons' meeting when they are asked by another church either to visit for an interview by the pastor search committee or when they are asked by the same committee to preach before the congregation in view of a call. Other pastors tell a few key leaders in their church when they are invited to visit churches for the above reasons. Some ministers announce the above to their congregations, and others publish such information in their bulletins. A few pastors even announce where they will be visiting and/or preaching and that if the church calls them they will accept.

Why do some pastors announce in advance that they will be visiting and/or preaching at another church? A few have told me they believe in being completely open with their members. Others feel it is ethical to do so. Often a pastor will announce such information to his congregation and ask them to make it a matter of prayer. While the reasons given above have validity, I personally do not believe it is wise to reveal this information to a church when the pastor goes to another church to visit, interview the pastor search committee or staff, or to preach in view of a call for the following reasons:

● If a pastor makes frequent contacts and/or visits to pastorless churches just to let his congregation beg him to stay or to use such invitations as a ploy to get something he wants from his people or to be more appreciated, such ventures and unorthodox schemes ought to be greatly discouraged or even accepted for what they are: schemes, unjustified ones at that.

● A pastor's visit to a pastorless church even in good faith and after much prayer should not be equated with a call to that church, unless of course the pastor search committee has made it clear initially that the committee has been authorized to extend a call to that pastor without a church vote. This happens in a few cases but not many. Most churches look upon a church voting in business session as the only call to a pastor. Thus, if a pastor visits a prospective church—or even preaches—and such a visit is not synonymous with a call, why burden a congregation with speculations?

● Perhaps the strongest reason for the pastor not to tell his congregation about going to a church for a visit or in view of a call is because no one can be absolutely positive what a church will do when it actually comes down to a vote. Even when a pastor search committee has done its "homework" and everything is A-OK, the call is not issued until that vote is taken and it is in the affirmative. The point is this: if the church does not issue a call because of an insufficient vote, the prospective pastor becomes a "lame duck" to his present congregation. In the church, as well as politics, a "lame duck" is a leader who has virtually lost his influence. Varied explanations to the pastor's people do not erase the painful truth of rejection.

I have known a few pastors who told their congregations they were going to certain churches to preach in view of a call with almost certain assurance from the pastor search committee that they would receive practically a unanimous vote to become pastor. In every case I have known where the vote was insufficient to issue a call, those pastors experienced an embarrassment and hurt they found extremely difficult to overcome. Some of those pastors felt they lost part of their effectiveness as they continued to minister to their congregation. While many congregations are gracious enough to understand the depressed feelings of their pastors after such discouraging experiences, other church members feel that they (the church members) are rejected by their pastors for "being put on trial" in the first place.

I know one minister who was considered by a church as pastor. The pastor search committee was unanimous in recommending him to the church in view of a call. He was so positive, from what the pastor search committee had told him, that he announced it to his church before the vote was taken. His wife even told her employer that she would be leaving. When the church that was to call him voted, the percentage was not sufficient according to the constitution, and he was devastated. His wife had to tell her employer that they were not leaving, and she would like to keep her job. The pastor's church had to be told what happened. His ministry suffered such a blow that he ultimately left without a place to go.

A simplistic answer to the congregation after a pastor allows his name to be presented to another church and does not receive sufficient votes to be called is, "Well, it just was not God's will for me to go to that church." I like to think that this is the actual valid reason why pastors do not receive enough votes when they are recommended by pastor search committees. Still this does not remove the feelings of a partial rejection in the minds of some in the present congregation. Nor does it erase the thought that more than likely the congregation would not have known about the vote had the pastor not announced it before it occurred. The old adage, "Don't count your chickens until they hatch," could well be compared to the above discussion. The spouse should *not* pack until the vote has been taken and the call is issued.

I do not think a pastor is deceiving a congregation when he does not reveal a matter as uncertain as a church voting on a pastor. However, every pastor has to make his own judgment "to tell or not to tell."

8
The Church's Expectations of the Pastor

One of the most difficult challenges facing the average pastor today is the unusually high expectations imposed on him by the members of his church congregation. To many people he is supposed to be a sort of superman—to know how to solve every problem of his members but never to have any problems of his own that he himself cannot solve. The difficulty is compounded by the notion that the minister himself has practically talked himself into believing he is supposed to be superhuman. And when he doesn't measure up to his own expectations he feels guilty, as if he has failed. Thus, when he can neither meet the superhuman expectations of his members or achieve his own unrealistic self-imposed goals of perfection, the minister lowers his own self-esteem. And the cycle seems to become endless.

Precious few people really understand the role of the pastor. They want him to wear "too many hats." He and his family do live in a "glass house." Many expectations the members have of their pastors are unreasonable; others are quite normal and necessary. The pastor knows when he accepts the call of God and the responsibility of a local church that he will be in the limelight almost constantly. What he does and says will to a large degree be looked upon as an example, good or bad, and how the pastor meets these expectations will have a heavy bearing on how he gets along with his members.

First, let's look at what the members should not expect of a prospective pastor.

Needless to say the list will be limited here, but the pastor in reality probably feels the expectations are limitless.

● They should not expect you to possess "all of the gifts of the

Spirit." If one minister could possess all of the good qualities, characteristics, and spiritual gifts that the average pulpit committee desires that pastor would be a "miracle man." But most committees do want far more than the average pastor can deliver.

It would be wonderful if every church could call a pastor who rates A+ in preaching, administration, promotion, organization, visiting, crisis ministry, counseling, finances, teaching, and good personality traits. But there are few, if any, pastors in this category.

No one person can excel in all of the gifts of the Spirit as listed in 1 Corinthians 12 and Romans 12. Even if such a pastor should suddenly appear on the scene with all the above qualities, every church in the country would want him.

When a pastor search committee contacts you and begins to show some genuine interest in you as pastor, be very frank in discussing their expectations. Let them know your strong points and assure them that you will seek to do your best in the areas where you are not as strong. If you give the committee the impression that you are gifted in areas where you know you are weak, you will probably live to regret it when they become disillusioned with your failures. Do not discuss all of your abilities. People like to be surprised to find that their pastor can do some things they did not anticipate.

• Also, they should not expect the pastor to be "the perfect pastor." By this, I mean it is not fair for the church members to put their pastor on a pedestal and when he falls or makes a mistake to lower their respect for him.

There should not be a double standard. But many members do want that double standard. They expect the pastor to "live a little better" than they are willing to live. Also, this applies to the pastor's family.

When a pastor goes to another church and begins a new ministry, he could say to the congregation, "I will try to be the best pastor I can be. I am human, and I will make mistakes. But I ask for your understanding and forgiveness when I do make blunders. In our pilgrimage together, as pastor and people, I ask that we walk together as people of God, striving daily to be more like the Christ who brought us together."

I did say something very similar to this at the beginning of my pastorates. I think it helps. It lets the people realize that we do have feet of clay, and it gives a good rapport with the people. It is not an apology or a sign of weakness. It is a plea for the acceptance of our humanity.

● Furthermore, the committee should not expect the pastor to be able to avoid personal crises just because he is "a holy man of God." He may have family problems just like the other members of the church. Being ordained ministers does not give us an automatic immunity from conflict or misunderstandings.

While it is true that ministers should not be called to a church "to be ministered unto, but to minister," it should be understood that they and their families need to be loved and understood. Pastors and their families need somebody to love them besides God. They need a human hand to reach out to them. When they hurt, they need to be able to cry and express their grief just like anyone else.

I would like to encourage every pastor and pastor's family to read Lucille Lavender's book, *They Cry Too.*[1] And when a pastor goes to a new church, it would be wise for him to encourage his people to read the same book. He could say, "Your understanding of my humanity, and that of my family, will be greatly appreciated and will bless our work together." He could donate a copy of this book to the church library.

● Next, let us take a look at the matter of the availability of a pastor. Some church members seem to feel that the pastor should be in the right place at the right time seven days a week. This is an expectation impossible to meet. It is true that pastors are "on call" twenty-four hours a day. Even on their "days off," they still must take care of emergencies and funerals. But often people will make pastors feel guilty when they indicate to them that they should have been at a certain place at a certain time when it was impossible to be there.

I recall how a pastor friend and I were sitting at a table in a restaurant one morning taking a coffee break. While we were talking, one of his church members walked by the table and "chewed him out" for wasting his time on a coffee break when his son, who had gotten into some trouble, needed a pastor to counsel with him at that very moment. After his member left our table, my pastor friend related how he had spent many hours trying to help that same young man. But what the father tried to do was lay a guilt trip on his pastor for not being in two places at the same time, an impossibility. He was also transferring his own hostilities and guilt to his pastor.

Second, what a pastor search committee and church do have a right to expect of a prospective pastor.

The average pastor search committee wants to find the best pastor possible. They not only want to be led by the Holy Spirit to find "a servant of God," but they want to make sure they are doing everything humanly possible to find the one who will be "just right" for their church.

The prospective pastor needs to realize that the pastor search committee may or may not know how to contact, hear, and deal with a prospective pastor. But the pastor search committee does have a right and responsibility to find out certain things about a potential pastor before he is called by the church they represent.

1. The committee has a right to want and receive biographical information (a resumé) on a prospective pastor before they hear him preach.

2. The committee has a right to consider a man on the basis of more than "one trial sermon." Committees are investigating prospective pastors more now than they did several years ago. They are encouraged to investigate personal character as well as pastoral or church records. No pastor should ever object to such investigation if he wants to stay in the ministry.

3. A pastor search committee has a right, as well as an obligation, to ask questions about a prospective pastor's work and beliefs, and to receive some positive answers. Also, they have a right and obligation to discuss matters about numerous areas. Some of the matters they may want to discuss are as follows:

His conversion, his call to the ministry, his sermon preparation, his concept of ministry, his support of missions, how he feels about the denomination and Christian education, his witnessing to the lost, current books he is reading, how he feels about youth and senior citizens, his concept of working with a staff, how he works with the church organizations, his relationship to the deacons, how he manages his time, strengths and weaknesses in his work, how he spends his time with his family, how his wife feels about her husband's call and work, his children.

(4) And, as already discussed, while the pastor's humanity ought to be understood, at the same time he ought to possess certain indisputable qualities, characteristics, and priorities such as the following:

- He must have a "second birth," of course—and know it.
- He must have a divine call from God—and know it.
- He must be able to relate to people—one on one and with a group.
- He must be a spiritual leader, one who will be respected in his capacity.
- He should be an example in holy living and moral conduct.
- He should maintain a good financial record.
- It is essential for a pastor to have a deep love for people, especially his members who call him to be an undershepherd, and he should be willing to visit in their homes when needed.
- His heart and soul should stay warm and compassionate for the unsaved, the sick, and bereaved as he makes his way to minister and witness to them.
- He should give enough of his time to organization and administration to keep the organism alive and healthy, but not so much time that he neglects other areas of his ministry.
- He should cooperate with the association and the convention in the denominational work concerning the mission and missions of the church.
- A pastor should be pastor of "all" people.
- Without apology, God's undershepherd must put integrity above expediency, never manipulating people for personal gain.
- Above all, he must be a man of prayer and a student of God's Word. The church has a right to expect God's man to study and be prepared to preach and teach His Holy Word. When

people come to the Lord's house they have a right to hear a "prepared sermon" on what God has to say, helping them meet the needs of everyday living. A pastor should keep his people "drinking out of a running stream instead of a stagnant pool."

- Also, a pastor should take care of himself physically, taking some time away from the tension of his work to get proper exercise and diversion. An adequate amount of this diversion ought to include activities with his family, knowing that family responsibilities are as much a part of his ministry as church activities.

- As he advances in age and tenure at any church, the pastor must work at staying optimistic and positive in his attitude, work, and association with his members and fellow workers.

What About the Church's Future Expectations of Ministers?

It is my personal opinion that the expectations of church members for pastors will increase rather than decrease. There was a time when churches had real difficulty in finding pastors to fill their pulpits. That picture has changed drastically over the last twenty-five years.

For example, the year I took my first full-time pastorate out of seminary, 1950, there was less than one clergy (0.8) for each church in my own denomination. Twenty-seven years later, only a year after I took my present position, 1977, there were over one and one-half (1.6) per church.

Even though anything can happen to change the oversupply of ministers, Carroll and Wilson, using the *Yearbook of American and Canadian Churches,* project that my denomination will have 2.6 clergy to each church by the year 2000.[2]

These projections use the straight-line extrapolations from the trends of the past quarter of a century. However, these writers make it emphatically clear that too much can happen over the next few years for such projections to come true. But they do state that these straight-line projections serve two functions: first, they call attention to the dramatic direction of past trends; second, they do alert us to the changes that must take place in the future if we do not want a repeat of these past trends. And these writers say, "We do not expect these projections to become facts."[3] But we do need to remember that these projections could become a reality. With our various seminaries crowded, and with the larger numbers of women being enrolled in these institutions year by year, the reality looks increasingly true.

You will notice from the table below[4] that the ratios of increase are pretty much the same in several other denominations except for the United Methodist Church.

DENOMINATIONS	RATIO OF CLERGY[b] TO CHURCHES		
	1950	1977	2000
Church of God (Anderson)	0.8	1.3	1.6
Church of Nazarene	1.3	1.6	1.8
Disciples of Christ	1.1	1.5	2.5
Episcopal Church	0.9	1.7	2.5
Lutheran Church in America	0.9[c]	1.3	2.0
Presbyterian, US	0.8[c]	1.3	2.0
Reformed Church in America	1.2	1.7	2.2
Southern Baptist Convention	0.8	1.6	2.6
United Church of Christ	1.0[c]	1.5	2.1
United Methodist Church	0.6[c]	0.9	1.0
United Presbyterian Church, USA	1.1	1.6	2.1

[b]Total Clergy, including retired
[c]1951 data

When churches are pastorless now, it is not unusual for the chairperson of the pastor search committee to receive a "superabundance" of names from many sources, without solicitation. And it is rather common now for committees working through a church-ministers relations office to ask for a second or third group of resumés on available pastors. I am aware that some of these churches have been caught in the inflation squeeze, and their expectations for a certain kind of pastor far exceed their ability to provide financial compensation equal to their desires or demands. But at the same time, some of the smaller churches which have just been contented to settle for "a preacher" in the past now want "a pastor" with the "indisputable qualities, characteristics, and priorities" I have mentioned in the preceding pages.

I have had a number of young men to say to me, "Why can't I get a church? I'm totally discouraged. I gave up a good job to go to seminary to prepare myself for ministry. My wife and children made a sacrifice for me to get through school." At the same time, I am well aware that many churches are without pastors, and the members will say, "If we have such a large number of ministers, why can't our church get a pastor?"

I repeat, many fine churches have difficulty in securing pastors because inflation has "priced them out of the market." And some of those fine churches have gone to bivocational pastors, thus decreasing the number of churches available for full-time pastors living on the church fields. This means the churches that remain full-time have even a larger pool of ministers from which to draw, and they can be more selective. Add to this trend the fact that more seasoned pastors are staying in their pastorates past age sixty-five and more retired ministers are serving "the second time around." Also, many retired ministers and other ordained men are serving as interim pastors for longer periods of time. In my own denomination, the job situation is more pronounced in those traditional areas of Southern Baptist strength, such as the South and the Southwest.

All of the above trends mean less church members for more clergy since the number of church members has not kept pace with the increase in clergy. For example, in my own denomination there were 317.6 members per clergy in 1950 and 235.6 in 1977.[5] The same holds true of most other denominations listed in this chapter. However, new churches will be organized every year. Isn't it reasonable to assume that the churches' expectations will be higher? Every church wants a pastor who is not only qualified but dedicated to a ministry of caring and serving.

The future expectations of the churches do not in any way limit the leadership of the Holy Spirit. If God wants you at a certain church at a certain time, He can provide "the will and the way." Bear in mind that the Holy Spirit uses human instruments, sources, and circumstances. By understanding this, every minister who wants to be a pastor, or change pastorates, should be ready when He calls.

9
The Pastor's Expectations of the Church

When a pastor search committee visits your church for the first time, or only time, you as a pastor would like to meet them and talk with them after the worship hour. But that may not happen, and you should not be too disappointed (unless they had called in advance and asked to meet with you after they heard you preach). In fact, any pastor search committee has a right to visit any church and hear any pastor without any obligation on the part of either party. Hearing a pastor preach should never be interpreted by any pastor as synonymous with the desire of that pastor search committee to call that speaker as pastor.

However, when a committee makes contact with a prospective pastor, hears him preach, and shows definite signs of interest in considering him as their pastor, that pastor does have a right to expect certain things from the committee. What are those expectations?

1. First, and foremost, you should expect them to pray and be led by the Holy Spirit. If they are just "looking for a preacher," they may be tempted to settle for the one who preaches the best sermon. You do not want that kind of church. You want to go to a new church with the definite feeling of the leadership of the Holy Spirit on the part of the committee and yourself.

2. The committee should know their church and community and be able to intelligently discuss both with a prospective pastor.

The Greek philosopher Socrates said, "Know thyself." Also, he said, "The unexamined life is not worth living." Surely this must be true with a church—the *ekklesia,* "the called-out ones." How can a committee adequately project a proper image of its local church to a prospective pastor unless it knows the life of the church?

The committee should have adequate knowledge in at least three areas in the life of the church:

(1) A brief history of the church. This should include such knowledge as the date of the establishment of the church, the periods of the greatest numerical growth, the factors that caused the growth (or decline), the giving record, the missionary outreach, how the church members have cooperated with the denominational programs, the general relationship of the members to one another, the average tenure of the pastors in the past few years and the circumstances under which they left.

(2) The present ministry of the church. The committee should take into consideration: the organizational leadership of the church (strengths and weaknesses), membership growth or decline, mission programs and support, church attendance, church stewardship, and ministry through witness and visitation programs.

(3) The future of the church and community. They should know the industrial and/or economic situation in the community or area. Is the church in a stable or drastically "changing community"? How are the other churches ministering? What type of ministry does the church hope to have? What about future needs of building/equipment? Is there need for additional staff positions? How can the missions program be improved? What other goals does the church have? What are the other needs? How does the church feel about change, creativity, or innovative ideas?

All three of the above areas are important in relationship to the type pastor the church needs at the present time. God has a certain person for a certain church at a certain time.

3. The committee should have some idea of what kind of pastor their church needs at this particular time in the life of the church. Do they need:

● An outstanding pulpiteer? An extremely strong administrator? More of a pastor type?

● Are they in need of a new building and want a pastor who will see them through a building program?

• Is there a large number of senior adults in the church? This would mean that they would need a pastor to set up a good program for this age group.

• Sometimes a committee will say, "Our church organizations really need some immediate attention. We want our next pastor to help get us back on the organization track."

The committee must know what kind of pastor is needed. And every pastor cannot meet every church's needs.

• Is the church looking for a conformist—one who just does what the members want him to do? James Glasse calls this type pastor one who has "the *conform/complaint syndrome*" when it comes to his problems.[1] *Syndrome* to Glasse is employed to mean "a group of signs and symptoms that appear together, and characterize a disease."[2] He says pastors with this conform/complaint syndrome will do something they know in advance is irrelevant, useless, stupid, or a waste of time, but most of the time they do this because someone asked them to do it. Then after the task is done, they will complain to somebody—usually the spouse—telling how they wasted their time. In other words, they conformed to their members' expectations, explained why it was necessary, then complained about it. Pastors do not break the syndrome, says Glasse, because they are such "expert explainers and complainers."[3] Are you a conformist?

Glasse pleads for ministers to break out of this syndrome and become change agents,[4] moving from the "passive-dependent" and adoptive stance to that of disciplines that will test their tolerance for change.

Are you a "change agent"? Or are you looking for a church where you can just do housekeeping, a sort of maintenance pastor —never taking any risks in ministry but just committed to the status quo?

4. The prospective pastor should expect the pastor search committee to give an honest and open appraisal or picture of the condition of the church. The committee should be willing to discuss with the prospective pastor such subjects as the following: the unity of the church, why the last pastor left, if the pulpit in the church is free (freedom to preach as God leads), the church staff

(if they have one), and future staff needs, support of missions and the Cooperative Program, the church's concept of the work of the pastor, the growth potential, the witnessing program, the church plant, the strongest program of the church, the weakest program of the church, and the greatest thing the church has done in the last ten years.

• Lyle Schaller has posed a question that ought to be asked to every pastorless church by every prospective pastor: "What is the purpose of this congregation meeting at this geographical location at this point in history? What do the members believe the Lord is calling their parish to do and to be? All parties should be prepared and willing to discuss purpose in terms of function, program, mission, and role, as well as in traditional theological clichés."[5]

The committee should be quite candid with the prospective pastor about any subject relating to the life and work of the church. It is far better to know the facts about a church before accepting the call to become pastor than to be shocked and depressed at the condition of the church after becoming pastor.

5. The pastor search committee should never promise a pastor more than the church can deliver. This would include matters relating to housing, additional staff members when and if needed, cost of living raises, benefits, service ministries, and any other related items. Many times pastor search committees will spend long hours seeking to find a pastor. They experience many disappointments. Often in their eagerness to secure a pastor for the church, they will make commitments to the prospective pastor without church approval only to find out later that the "goods could not be delivered."

The prospect should feel free to ask such questions as these: "Has the church or the proper committee approved this matter? If not, would you please check this out and let us discuss it again?"

6. The prospective pastor has a right to expect the committee to take the initiative in discussing "money matters" and other benefits. The pastor has a right to expect a good salary. The amount should be large enough to deliver him from financial burdens that would hamper his ministry. (And, pastor, start your retirement program *early* in your ministry. Encourage the committee and the

church to begin and/or participate in an annuity program for you. Talk with your state convention annuity representative. Get him/her to talk with your church about the urgency of participating in this program.)

I recently heard a pastor say braggingly, "Why I didn't even know what my salary would be until I moved on the church field!" That is nothing to brag about. That is not faith; that is a lack of planning and is poor business.

God-called men are not in the ministry for money, but it does take money to meet the financial responsibilities, and the "labourer is worthy of his hire."

Being pastor of a church is a great privilege and a tremendous responsibility. You, as a prospective pastor, have a right to expect enough information from the pastor search committee in order that the Holy Spirit may guide you to make the right decision.

10
When a Pastor Search Committee Invites and Presents You to Its Church in View of a Call

When a committee invites you to its church in view of a call, it ought to be one of the climatic stages of their search and "homework." It's not the final one, of course, but it's a stage very much like an engagement of a couple before the wedding takes place. So both parties, pastor and committee, need to know the seriousness of the visit.

The church that invites you to visit in view of a call may not be the traditional-type church that has a Sunday "trial sermon." It may be a church that hears a prospective pastor on large video screens from video tapes the committee has obtained from the prospective pastor. These video tapes may be sermons the prospect has preached in his present church on various Sundays in the past. The committee may designate a certain week night and invite the entire church membership to come to specified rooms in the church building to hear these prerecorded videotapes of the prospective pastor's sermons. Following the showing of the tapes the membership could be invited to a reception to meet the prospect in person. Then the church would have an opportunity to vote on him at a later time (maybe the following Sunday) but without the typical Sunday "trial sermon" and without the prospect being present.

However, many pastors would not accept a church without preaching a trial sermon. They want to get the "feel" of the congregation—and to a large degree the church is on trial as much as the prospective pastor.

On the other hand, the prospective pastor may be invited to follow the "traditional procedure" of the vast majority of churches that hear a "trial sermon" on Sunday morning. The church would probably want to give a church-wide reception for the prospect on Saturday evening so every member would have an opportunity to meet him before he preaches the trial sermon on the next morning.

Regardless of which procedure is used, one thing ought to be clear: all signals must be "go" before the prospective pastor is ever presented to the church.

When it is possible, as stated previously, it is wise for the prospective pastor to visit the church building on a separate occasion and meet some of the leaders of the church before the people hear him preach. Certainly he should be given a tour of the community or city by a committee member to see places of interest (such as schools, subdivisions, industries, or farms) and get a general overview of the whole situation.

If the pastor has children should they accompany the pastor and spouse on that first visit or when the pastor preaches? I personally believe it would be advantageous for the couple to have a baby-sitter or take them to relatives if the children are small. The parents would certainly be under less tension and pressure. However, if the children are teenagers I believe they should be given the choice to stay with friends or go with the parents.

There are some things of extreme importance that ought to be taken care of *before* the prospective pastor preaches and is presented to the congregation in view of a call:

1. I think the prospective pastor should have a great deal of interest in the church and the possibility of ministry there before he consents to let the people hear him preach in view of a call.

2. Also, I would want to know that the pastor search committee is unanimous in its recommendation of the prospective pastor to the church. If a small committee cannot be in full agreement that you are God's servant it wants as its pastor, it is highly unlikely that the church would give an acceptable call.

3. If you have not done so already, be sure to have a very frank discussion with the committee about their expectations of a pastor.

4. There should be an honest and free discussion about a working schedule, office procedures, compensation, staff, and other

mutual things about pastor-church relations you have not already discussed. The time to do this with the committee is *before* you preach to the congregation. If the committee does not bring up the above items in your discussions and interviews, and you find out it does not plan to do so before you are presented to the church, it would be wise to say to them very tactfully, "I believe it would be better to put some kind of agreement in writing that we can present to the church." If such an agreement is not given to the people before you preach to the congregation, it ought to be mailed or given to every member *before they vote on you.*

5. I strongly urge that every member of the church should be informed about the visit of the prospective pastor when he is invited to visit the church and to preach. If he comes on a weekend and preaches on Sunday, a letter should be sent to every church family on Monday or Tuesday one or two weeks before the prospective pastor preaches the following Sunday.

The first page could be a picture of the prospective pastor and a message (letter) from the pastor search committee itself. The next page could give a brief biographical sketch of the prospective pastor. The third page could be a copy of the agreement the pastor search committee discussed with the prospective pastor during one or more of the interviews or discussions. The last page could be given to a schedule of events for the weekend.

Examples of the above are given at the end of this chapter so the pastors can know what the churches are encouraged to send out to every church family.

If the church hears the minister preach on Sunday and the congregation votes the very same day, I encourage the church to mail all pages of the letter, including the agreement. If the minister preaches on one Sunday and the church votes the following Sunday, the agreement could be mailed on the Monday after he preaches, along with a second letter from the committee, so every member would know exactly what agreement the committee had made with the prospective pastor. Giving an oral report to the members of the church immediately before the vote is taken is most undesirable and can bring about unnecessary misunderstandings. It is to the advantage of the church members *and* the prospective pastor for a *written agreement* to be in the hands of the church members in advance of the vote.

In cases where the church does not follow the traditional Sunday "trial sermon," the same materials should be sent, except for the fourth page dealing with the time element and the "weekend" schedule. The fourth page then would tell of the videotapes and the visit of the prospect during a weekday. And the letter would be sent several days earlier.

Then, of course, one of the most important aspects of the visit is the sermon the prospective pastor will preach to the congregation.

1. Preach a message you know God is leading you to preach, and preach something you will feel comfortable preaching. Be sure it is fresh to you and can be preached with a warm feeling and enthusiasm. Remember, regardless of how hard you may try, you will still be under more pressure and strain than if you were preaching in your own pulpit (under normal conditions).

● Avoid preaching on an unusually controversial subject. There will be plenty of time to do this if you are called to the church.

● Also, I believe the prospect would show wisdom by preaching in the positive instead of the negative. People are hungry to know what God can do to help them. They hear enough "don'ts" without a visiting minister adding another set to their list.

● Go to the pulpit with confidence in God's leadership and in yourself. You are what you think. If you think you will do well for God's glory, you will. If you expect to fail you probably will not be disappointed.

● Try your best to be yourself. If you are by nature a humorous person, the humor will come through. But if you are not humorous and you try to be on that given Sunday, you may regret trying.

● Since we live in a "time-conscious age" when people "punch in and punch out" when they go to work, be aware of their time in your preaching. Dr. R. G. Lee could preach an hour and keep the interest and attention of the congregation. Unless you feel that you are another great orator, try to get through with your sermon before the people do. If you have a lot more to say, it may keep long enough for you to say it if you become their pastor.

2. If possible, the visiting minister should speak at both the morning and evening worship hours.

I'm aware that all churches will not do the above things. Some churches would not be financially able to do them. Other churches would not want to do them even if they were able to do so. A few churches would not even want to have a fellowship hour in the building and serve refreshments. Many churches would only expect to meet and hear a prospective pastor when he preaches on Sunday morning.

Prior to the prospective pastor's coming, it would be helpful for the committee to send out a mailing which would include a letter, a biographical sketch of the prospective pastor, and an agreement on compensation (salary, benefits, allowances, vacation, and the like). Here follow examples of such a report to the church:

A REPORT TO EAST CHURCH
200 Green Street
Anywhere City, USA
By the Pastor Selection Committee
Robert T. Dogood, Chairman
Evelyn B. Upright
John T. Service
Sarah R. Busy
William D. Cares

We, the members of the pastor search committee, deeply appreciate the confidence placed in us by the church in such a vital matter.

We have humbly sought the leadership of the Lord as we searched for the right person to lead us as pastor of our church.

We have felt the power of your prayers during the weeks of investigation, prayer, and travel. We appreciated the response of the membership when we asked for your input as to the type of minister our church should seek. Your suggestions had a definite bearing on the direction of the committee.

We are confident of the leadership of the Holy Spirit in this decision. Unanimously, we feel that God has truly led us to the right person in Reverend Jim B. Goode, and we would like to have you know more about him. The information which follows will introduce you to this person whom we plan to recommend as pastor of the East Church.

Biographical Sketch

The Reverend Jim B. Goode was born in New Town, USA, on August 10, 19____. He graduated from _____ University in 19____ with a B.A. degree. He also graduated from _____ Seminary in 19____ with a M. Div. degree.

Reverend Goode was licensed and ordained by the _____ Church in _____, USA.

He pastored the Little Chapel Church in _____ and the Green Memorial Church in _____ while he was in college and seminary. Since completing his formal education, he has pastored the following churches:

19____ to 19____ - West Side Church _____

19____ to 19____ - Downtown Church _____

19____ to 19____ - Northside Church _____

He is presently pastor of the Southside Church in _____, where he has served since 19____.

Reverend Jim B. Goode has served in numerous positions in the various associations and state conventions. From 19____ to 19____ he was a member of the trustees of _____ University. Last year he served as president of the _____ Convention. He has written articles for the various state papers and is a regular contributor to such magazines as *Church Administrator,* and *The Deacon.* He is a popular speaker for youth retreats.

Reverend Goode is married to the former Ruth _____ of Old Town, _____. She is a graduate of _____ College. The Goode's have two children: Ben B. Goode and Wilma B. Goode.

An Agreement

The following details have been agreed upon by the pastor search committee and Reverend Jim B. Goode. These items are a part of the recommendation from the pastor search committee.

1. Compensation
   (1) Base Salary . . . . Amount. . . . . $____
       Housing:
          Pastorium____Annual Fair Market Val.____
          or

Housing Allowance . . . .   _____
Utilities Allowance . . . .   _____
Total Salary $_____

(2) Benefits
Retirement percentage:_____ . . . . $_____
Group Life & Long-Term Disability Ins. _____
Medical-Hospitalization . . . .   _____
Other, that is, Social Security . . . . . .   _____
(Note: Ordained ministers considered
self-employed for Social Security.)
Total Benefits $_____

(3) Service Ministries (Nonsalary)
Car Expenses. . . . . $_____
Convention Expenses . . . .   _____
Books & Continuing Education. . . . . .   _____
Other . . . .   _____
Total Service Ministries $_____

(If the church gives a housing allowance instead of furnishing a pastorium, which ought to be encouraged where feasible, the following item should be included in this agreement: "It shall be the pastor's responsibility to secure housing within the church community [if possible].")

2. It shall be the responsibility of the church to pay moving expenses from the pastor's present home to his new home in our community.

3. The church will pay expenses for the pastor to the following conventions and seminars, including pulpit supplies for the Sundays involved: (list here)

4. The pastor is to have four (4) weeks paid vacation annually, with the church paying the pulpit supplies for the four Sundays involved.

5. The pastor shall have the privilege of conducting a maximum of four (4) revivals or conferences away from the church annually, with the church paying the pulpit supplies.

6. We encourage the pastor to take the privilege of having one day off a week. He shall have the opportunity of choosing which day.

Please Note: Some churches are now giving a pastor a sabbatical after he has been at the church from five to seven years. This means the pastor may take some time off from the church for indepth refreshing study to help replenish his body, soul, and mind to be a better pastor. The church can set the amount of time and, of course, his salary would continue as usual, with the church paying for the pulpit supplies during his absence. This arrangement will be a blessing to both the pastor and the church.

Some churches who furnish a pastorium to a pastor instead of providing a housing allowance are setting aside a monthly amount of money in a savings account in the pastor's name as a down payment for a future home. Since many fine pastors spend a lifetime in various pastoriums, they reach retirement without a place to live.

Include any other agreements and list them below.

11

How Can You Tell When or If It Is the Right Church for You?

When a pastor is invited to preach before a church congregation in view of a call, how can he tell if it is or is not the right church for him? There is no magic formula to follow to know when it is right to accept a new challenge. I do believe there are some guidelines to help pastors.

● First and foremost, one must rely on the leadership of the Holy Spirit to find God's will in such a matter. Without His aid a pastor will simply stumble in the dark.

● Second, remember that the Holy Spirit does not work alone. He expects the pastor to use common sense and sound judgment. So do not impose on the Holy Spirit to give you an answer without some human effort on your part. So:

1. Learn all you can about the church before you let them vote on you.

(1) What about the *history* of the church? Did it get a good start? How long have the pastors stayed there? Why did most of them leave? How did they accept and treat their pastors? Have they been mission minded? How have the organizations of the church functioned? What kind of outreach have they had?

(2) What is the church doing *now* besides just meeting for study and worship? What about their evangelistic and mission outreach? Are the various organizations functioning well? Is the church community in a state of decline or growth?

(3) Are the leaders of the congregation excited about the *future* of their church? What are some of their goals? Are they ready for a new pastor? Do you get the feeling that the people care about people and want to help meet their needs?

2. Now in the light of the church itself how do you feel that your spiritual gifts can help meet the needs of the people? Are the needs of the church your weakest or your strongest gifts of the Spirit in ministry? For example, for years their church has been known for and built on a strong pulpit ministry. Is this one of your strongest gifts of the Spirit? What if the weakest area of your ministry is organization and promotion, and the pastor search committee feels this is one of the greatest needs of their church? There are many other areas of importance in the use of one's gifts too. The point is: Would the church members reach their potential with the use of your gifts of the Spirit as their leader?

3. What is your own personal background and training? It is extremely important for you to be compatible with a future congregation. If you and the congregation are poles apart in too many areas, it would affect both your happiness and the spiritual growth and happiness of the church. So here are some areas you might want to consider:

(1) Are you oriented to a certain geographical area of the country and have a mind-set for working with people who mainly think and talk like you? Would any prejudice you might have for other cultural and ethnic groups impair your ministry to the extent that you know you would not be effective in ministry? A simple answer would be, "Well, if you love the Lord you can work anywhere and with any people." That may be true, but if incompatibility in the above areas reach a boiling point, an explosion may take place. You know who usually gets hurt. If God calls you to an area totally different from where you have served in the past, be sure you have buried (or will be willing to) any prejudice or "unwillingness to change" in an unmarked grave.

(2) What if you were born and reared in the big city and a pastor search committee from a rural church contacts you in view of a call? Would you be willing to adjust to rural life or has the urban life-style so imbedded itself into your mind and habits that you would be unhappy and even ineffective? Would you be willing to change to a slower pace and learn the ways of rural life? Or what if you were reared in a rural area and a church in the inner city

wants to call you as pastor? Would you be compatible in a totally different life-style?

Here again someone may say, "But when God calls a person to preach, one ought to be willing to go anywhere." I am not talking about preaching. I am not referring to one serving under the auspices of a mission board. I am referring to one serving as a pastor where there is not a "built-in tenure," and where one's program and ideas may be drastically and radically contrary to the people to whom one ministers.

(3) What about your educational background? The highly educated pastor who may be considered as pastor by a church where the average member has an extremely limited education may be wise to ask himself these questions: Will I be happy in such a church over a long period of time? Can I make my sermons clear enough to the people so they will understand the redemption offered by Christ and trust Him as Savior? Can or will I be willing to be patient and long-suffering in my preaching on discipleship to help them become mature Christians and church members?

What if your education is extremely limited and the members of the inquiring church are the opposite? Can you challenge them Sunday after Sunday over an extended period of time? Or will your new sermons be just a rehashing of the one or two messages they heard you preach as "trial sermons"?

I am not saying "minor leaguers" cannot play "major league" churchmanship; neither am I indicating that one capable of "major-league preaching" would be out of position on any church field. I am saying too many godly men have been called to churches that outgrew them educationally, then they were dismissed.

Someone may reply: Cannot the Holy Spirit overcome this imbalance between the pastor and the people regardless of how poorly or highly trained one or the other might be? Yes, the Holy Spirit can help the pastor and church overcome any difficulty. However, people often will not let the Holy Spirit guide them into a long-lasting relationship of pastor and people.

(4) What about your theological stance? Most pastor search committees will want to know what you believe about the Bible before they present your name in view of a call. Oh, yes, you and

the church believe the whole truth as proclaimed in the Word of God. But what if the church equates one's stand on millennialism (regardless of what position it might be) with one's spirituality? Suppose this becomes a test of fellowship in the church? How does the church's stand on the practice of baptism and the Lord's Supper match your beliefs? Learn enough about the theological beliefs of the congregation from the pastor search committee, so there will not be a constant clash of "theological incompatibility" if you should accept their church as pastor.

(5) How would your temperament fit into such a situation? If the church has a history of conflict and controversy, you might want to ask these questions:

a. Do you run from opposition and conflict, always thinking the grass is greener on the other side?

b. Does criticism have an adverse effect on your ministry to the extent that you stay depressed when it becomes severe?

c. Can you love people who do not love you or who always live in the negative? Some church congregations just have a more loving spirit than others. They seem to stay unified in spite of severe adversity. Do you have to be in such a fellowship of believers to survive in the ministry?

• Another area to consider is: Would your family be happy and compatible in the church that is considering you. I realize it is difficult to anticipate what the church might be and do down through the years. The pastor and his family ought to meet the members of the pastor search committee and know enough about the membership, the school situation, the location of the church building, the possibility of where they might live, and other areas of the church and community to at least get "the feel" of how things might be if the call is accepted.

• An important guideline too is the challenge the prospective church may offer. I am not referring to the size, outreach possibilities, or even the size of the budget. The challenge could be to unite a divided church. It may even be an inner-city church that needs just your type ministry.

• And what about the peace you have in your heart about leaving where you are and where you are going? Please do not confuse or equate the emotional trauma about leaving where you are with God's will for you to stay. You may not want to leave where you are now. Your personal desire may be to stay. If you do not have peace about staying because you do have peace about going to another place, that is a good indication God could be in the move.

• Too many good pastors have suffered agonizing years of ministry in places where they "thought God led them," only to find out later that their human desires to get a church, or change churches, led to a divorce with the church.

A young pastor who talked with me recently wants to leave the church where he has served as pastor for about a year. He has found out that his church people "do not want to do anything deeply spiritual." They merely want him to do housekeeping—preach but not get anybody disturbed or challenged enough to do anything for the Lord that would "rock the boat." This young man is a dynamic preacher, a wonderful soul-winner, and a well-educated minister with many gifts of the Spirit. He said he felt the Holy Spirit led him to his present church about a year ago. But now he says, "I know that I came more out of compassion than out of a divine call to the church." He said, "I do not fit into the life of this church. We are a mismatch." He remarked, "It would have been much better for the church and for me if I had considered many other factors than just my compassion for the people. I was so eager to minister in some church that I failed to take into account more than just the will of God. I sought the will of God in the call but did not consider other factors that would enter into my ministry at that church."

Do not blame the Holy Spirit if you should accept a church and then feel that a mistake was made in your going to that church. Two people can be in love and just know that they will have a successful marriage, then find out later that it takes more than just love to make a marriage work. Some marriages are mistakes in the very beginning. Some church and pastor relationships are a mistake in the very beginning.

Just be sure you do your part to let the Holy Spirit guide you in making your decision. You want to have a good relationship from the very beginning.

12
Voting on the Prospective Pastor

Voting to call a pastor is a very critical matter. If a church votes to call a pastor, and he declines, it creates a temporary crisis in the church. The pastor search committee often feels like they have been jilted, or at least they have failed. They feel this way especially when they have been led to believe that the prospect would accept if called.

On the other hand, if a church votes on a prospective pastor, and the vote is not sufficient to call him, the pastor has a temporary crisis—especially if his present church knows that another church is voting on him, or if they find it out later.

● For the above two reasons, I want to express two firm convictions I have about a church voting on a pastor.

One, a church should vote on a pastor *only* after he gives his approval and is almost 100 percent sure he would accept the call if the vast majority of the votes cast are in his favor and in keeping with the policies of the church. It would be wise for the church to delay the vote if the pastor is unsure about accepting the church. If after a reasonable time the pastor is still undecided, he should withdraw his name and not permit the church to vote on him.

Two, a pastor's name should not be presented to the church for a vote unless the entire pastor search committee feels the church membership would give the prospective pastor a vote sufficient to be called as pastor. The committee should, after lengthy discussions with the prospective pastor, know the heartbeat of the membership well enough to know the prospect would be well received. This does *not* mean the committee could give positive assurance to the prospect that he would be called. No one can ever predict exactly what a church will do when it comes to a vote. But the committee ought to be so representative of the church that they could pretty well know what direction the membership would take.

● When should the vote be taken? If the church has a constitution and bylaws, the committee would check them carefully concerning the procedure for calling a pastor. However, if the church does not have such a document, and the prospective pastor and the committee have both given their approval, the vote could be taken:

On the same Sunday after he preaches, or

On the following Sunday, or

On Wednesday night, either immediately following the Sunday he preaches or the following Wednesday night, or

At a given called business meeting.

● How should the vote be taken: Unless the constitution and bylaws specify a certain method, the church may choose from a number of ways: (1) a standing vote or by lifted hand, (2) voice vote, (3) by prepared ballot.

● What should be included in the recommendation when the church votes? I personally think it should include the following:

(1) It should state how the pastor search committee feels about calling the prospective pastor.

(2) The church should be asked to extend a call to the prospect to become pastor of the church.

(3) The call should include the "agreement" concerning the annual compensation and matters such as moving expenses, conventions, vacations, and any other items (as already discussed and mailed to every church family).

(4) The recommendation should include at least a summary of the church's expectations of the pastor and the pastor's expectations of the church (as discussed by the committee and prospective pastor during the various interviews and conferences prior to the extension of the call). This summary of a "Pastor-Church Covenant" should be made as a part of the call. The summary should state that the church establish a church-minister relations commit-

tee to help maintain and nurture this covenant. Such a committee could annually review and implement the covenant, and it could mediate any misunderstandings or conflicts that might arise.

The pastor search committee should state that such a covenant would not be a binding legal contract, but a statement of mutual understanding and perceptions, with a promise of continued love and respect for each other.

A summary of a "Pastor-Church Covenant" might be as follows:

Brother (or Reverend) _____ promises to be a trustworthy undershepherd, endeavoring to understand, love, and care for those entrusted to his spiritual care, and to recognize the work with the congregation's elected leaders. He has stated that he would commit himself to practice a life-style spiritually, morally, and financially that will reinforce his role as a spiritual leader and guide to others. He has promised to maintain competency in ministry through diligent Bible study and sermon preparation, dependence on the Holy Spirit for leadership, provide administrative and organizational leadership, and grow in pastoral and prophetic skills through continued study.

The Church's Commitment

We have agreed with the prospective pastor that we, as a church congregation, will commit ourselves to respect and honor the office our new pastor will hold, trusting him as a person of integrity and ability and that we will not only love him as our pastor, but we will love him and accept him as a fellow human being.

We will give him freedom in the pulpit to express honest, thoughtful convictions in interpreting God's Word though they may not always coincide with those of every individual in the congregation.

We will undergird our new pastor's ministry with daily prayer and with a positive and loving attitude. We will do our best to shelter our pastor's family with affectionate care and freedom for personal growth and expressions of their own unique personalities and gifts.

We extend this call with a promise to provide for our pastor's

adequate financial needs in the future and to show appreciation for
his fruitful areas of ministry.

• A written copy of the above recommendation should be presented to the pastor if called by the church.

• What percentage of the vote should the prospective pastor
receive before accepting the call? He would certainly want to
receive a substantial majority vote before accepting the call. I think
it is unwise for the prospective pastor to tell the committee that
it absolutely must be unanimous before he would accept. Even
telling a committee that the vote must be 90 or 95 percent before
he would accept would be unwise also. Suppose a prospective
pastor makes such a statement before the vote is taken, and then
he accepts the call even if it is 80 percent? Would this reflect on
a man's integrity? Would such a change of mind impair a man's
ministry at that church in the very beginning? It would be better
to say to the committee, "Let us wait until after the vote is taken
to make a decision concerning the call." In that way, the prospect
and the committee are not putting limitations on the leadership of
the Holy Spirit. It is rather rare in most churches to get a unanimous vote.

• How long should the pastor take to reply to the committee if
the church votes to call him? Even though only the prospect himself can determine how long he should take, I would discourage
a prospective pastor from taking too much time. I have known
some cases where a pastor took several weeks. This is unfair to
both the church and the pastor.

13
Resignation and Closure at the Present Church

When another church has called you as pastor, two important things must be done: You must resign from your present church, and bring your ministry to a close at that location. Often such tasks are not easy, especially if you have been at your present pastorate for a long time and/or your roots are deep within the church and the community. The task is even doubly difficult when you have children who have developed deep friendships at church, school, and in the community.

1. Resigning.—Unless your situation is very unusual, it would probably be wise to inform your deacons before announcing it to the entire church. Use your own wise discretion as to the timing.

When you announce your resignation to the congregation it would be best to write it out and read it to the congregation. If it would be too difficult for you emotionally, get the chairman of the deacons to read it.

Here is a sample letter of resignation:

PASTOR'S LETTER OF RESIGNATION

The Members of ——————— Church
_____

My Dear People:

For the past five years it has been my privilege to serve as your pastor. These have been among the very happiest years of my life. You have been a loyal, cooperative, and understanding people. For the rest of my life, I shall hold in my memory a warm and affectionate place for the members of this fine church.

During these years as your pastor, I have constantly prayed and preached that the uppermost thing in our lives should be to seek and to do the will of God. So, conscientiously and sincerely, after much prayer and thought and with the firm conviction that I am following God's will, I offer my resignation as pastor of this church to accept a call to the pastorate of the _____ church of _____, _____ to become effective (date).

This has not been an easy or hasty decision. It has been one of the most difficult decisions of my life. My family will regret to leave as much as I. Our ministry among you will be cherished for the rest of our lives. I firmly believe that the future of this church is bright, and I shall ever rejoice to hear of your continual progress for the Master. May God continue His richest blessings upon each and every one of you.

Devotedly yours,

_____

(signature)

2. Bringing Your Ministry to a Close.—Once a pastor resigns from his present pastorate he becomes a "lame duck."

● How long should you stay after you resign? I have known some cases where a pastor would resign on one Sunday and not go back to the pulpit the next Sunday. I personally do not think this is fair to the congregation or to the pastor, even if the pastor does consider himself a "lame duck." However, it is not wise to stay too long after resigning. Some churches have constitutions that require a pastor to give a two or four weeks notice before leaving. Regardless of the time element, those closing days can be meaningful to both the pastor and the church.

● Keep ministering to the people as if you were spending the rest of your life there. Being a lame duck does not mean being a lazy duck. You are still pastor, and you have sermons to preach, members to visit, and other kinds of ministries.

● You may be asked to give guidance to the church concerning a pastor search committee. You might refer them to the State Church-Ministers Relations Office and the Director of Missions. However, it is very wise to let the church do their own selecting of the committee and to let them function on their own without trying to tell them what kind of pastor to call.

• If you have had some very unpleasant experiences at the church or if you have had some personality clashes with members of the church, do not let such experiences "get in your preaching" during those closing days. The pulpit is not the place to get rid of your hostilities, nor is it ethical to take advantage of your position to assassinate someone's character, even if he or she deserves it. Be positive in your preaching.

• If the church wants to give you and your family a farewell reception and/or a gift, accept it with grace and gratitude. Give the people who love you an opportunity to express it.

• Take every opportunity you have to express your appreciation for the privilege of serving the church as pastor. Leave the church with a good spirit on your part. Let the people know you love them.

• If you have a staff, express your appreciation to them before you leave. If things haven't always been pleasant in your staff relations, don't lose your cool when you leave.

• Do what you can to prepare the church for the next pastor. Some positive preaching about the role of the undershepherd could help. Also try to leave things in good order for the next pastor. Leave your keys to the building in an envelope. If you write a letter to your successor, welcome him to the church without naming any problems or problem people. Let him find out the good or bad features on his own. It would be unwise to prejudice him toward the church people or program in any way whatsoever.

• Do your best to prepare the church for the interim period. Stress the need for unity, visitation, witnessing, giving, attendance at the worship hours, and continued training. Encourage the people to support the entire church program and to work harder while the church is without a pastor. And by all means, ask the church to pray for the pastor search committee that God will lead them to the right pastor. Of course, assure the church of your prayers and interest for their future ministry, knowing that the greatest compliment you can receive is to know that the work you have done there will continue to be blessed of the Lord.

• When you move to your next pastorate, "turn loose" of the one you are leaving. If you make return visits, let them be infrequent. Be fair and considerate to your successor. Learn how to gracefully and ethically bow out.

When you leave a pastorate, you naturally leave a little bit of yourself there: good or bad. You can never completely forget the people to whom you ministered or the work to which you devoted so much of your life. So when you close your ministry at the church you are leaving, I hope both you, as pastor, and your members can say the words Calypso said to Ulysses when he was about to leave the enchanted isle where she lived, "Say goodbye to me, but not to the thought of me."

14
Pastorium or Housing Allowance

Years ago when a pastor was called to a new full-time pastorate, there was not much doubt about where he and his family would live: the pastorium. Things have drastically changed in the past few years. There is a good possibility that when you are called to your next pastorate, you may start house hunting.

Let us suppose that you will be given a housing allowance at your next church. Will this be your first purchase of a house? Do you have a down payment? Where will you borrow money? Do you know how and where to purchase a house?

On the other hand if the church that calls you has a pastorium, what will be the immediate advantages to you? Or, what if the church that calls you has a pastorium, but the committee has told you that the church has voted to give you the choice of either living in it or giving you a housing allowance?

These are some things I want to consider in this chapter. I want to be helpful to the pastor that may be in a dilemma about what to do.

1. Let's take the easy route and say the church owns a pastorium, and the pastor doesn't have a choice. What are the advantages of moving into the pastorium?

(1) The house is available immediately, and there is no "house hunting."

(2) If the church is "a pastor-caring church," they will provide a nice home, and they will refurbish it before your family moves into it. This should be discussed before you accept the call to the church.

(3) Most likely, the pastorium would be located within a reasonable distance to the church building.

(4) And, of course, you wouldn't have to worry about a down payment, repairs, or taxes. When or if you move to another church later, you wouldn't fret about the marketability of your home and be caught making two mortgage payments if the next church gives a housing allowance. Neither would you have the worry of having to "fix up and paint up" for resale.

2. But what if the new church gives a housing allowance, and you have to go "house hunting"? You might think about the following:

(1) It would be wise to pass the word along to your new church members, perhaps through the pastor search committee, that you will be looking for a certain size and type of house and if anybody knows of one for sale along that line to please let you know.

(2) Then find out through the committee what real estate agents they would recommend. If one is on the committee, you might feel free to use him or her but don't feel "stuck" with a realtor just because he or she is a member of your church. Get the best help you can. Use several sources. But whatever you do, choose a real estate agent: a "good" realtor. Be sure the realtor is competent. Choose one that has access to "multiple listing" of homes and whose business is "computerized" if possible. Make sure the realtor knows the various areas of the city or county where the most houses are located in your price range, and not one whose knowledge is limited to just one price range or community. And choose one who knows home values and financing. By all means, the realtor *must* have appraisal experience and know how to calculate to save you money. According to my good friend Pete Lunati, a successful realtor and owner of Pete Lunati Realty Company in Nashville, Tennessee, the real estate market is different in every area and also different in every subdivision in every city. So a realtor may know the market values in some areas but not be knowledgeable in other areas.

(3) Also, it will be important for you to talk with a good financial advisor about your financial needs. This person could be the realtor or someone else that might be highly recommended to you.

This financier can help you to know your options when you shop for financing and particularly what kind of mortgage programs are available in your new community. He may be able to talk with you about the computerized mortgage-listings services too. He will need to know your income, so you can discuss how much financing you can afford. How much will you need as a down payment? How much can you afford in monthly payments? As of this writing, the conservative leaders would recommend that your monthly house payment—principal, interest, taxes and insurance—should not exceed more than 28 percent of your gross monthly income. Please note:

If you own your home at your present pastorate, you might use the equity you have in it for a down payment, or as collateral.

But what if this is your first buy and you simply do not have any money as a down payment? What do you do then? Your financial advisor might suggest that:

You borrow on the cash value of your insurance policies.

If you should still need cash, perhaps you might get someone to take a second mortgage on your house and loan you additional money. This person might even be a relative.

Do not overlook the thought that many churches calling pastors will make loans to them, often interest free or at a lower interest rate, with the understanding that the loan would be paid back only when or if they leave. Sometimes a church will be even more generous than this, knowing that a pastor has lived in a pastorium for years and hasn't any equity in a home. Often even selling your home in one pastorate may not give you enough down payment in another area where real estate is substantially higher.

Now what about house hunting. Your realtor can direct you to houses within a reasonable distance of the church building. Or you may find that prices near your church are out of your ability to finance. The realtor would then help you reach a decision to buy farther away from the church to stay "within your means" and still get a good house.

Should your family house hunt with you? One realtor told me, "Never buy a house without your spouse seeing it first." Mr. Lunati said it would be great if your children could go with you when you "hunt." It will make them feel more a part of the decision to change churches. And house hunting could help relieve some of the trauma they will face in leaving their friends.

Consider some long-range plans when you buy a house. You may not get what you want when you buy your first house.

● It may be too old, too small, too expensive to heat and cool, or too far from the church building or schools. Think in terms of living there for at least two or three years (to at least cover the points you may pay on your loan), then sell and use the equity to purchase something a little more to your needs. Then the next time, you can move up again.

● Keep in mind that wherever you buy, *location* is extremely important. It may well determine the marketability when you need to sell.

What if you have the option of buying the pastorium at your new pastorate? Suppose the church wants out of the real estate business?

● Move with caution if you do this. Some members have a lot of sentiment toward any church property. And you don't want the members to feel like you are "taking advantage of them." If you sense this in any way, go in a different direction for a house— which may be better in the long run anyway. However, if the members want to sell the house, want you to have it, and make you an offer you "can't turn down," go ahead and purchase it.

What if the church has a pastorium, and you are told that you can live in it until you find a house you want to buy? A word of caution: just be sure the housing allowance is part of the written agreement so there will not be any misunderstanding when you move out of the pastorium.

Regardless of what you buy, talk with your realtor about important items to check before you buy, such as the adequacy of the house, a termite clause, the title and insurance policy. Of course, make sure that settlement costs are not excessive. Have a real estate attorney review all documents before settlement. Remember, too, that many aspects of the home-buying process are negotiable, such as who pays discount points—buyer or seller—that lenders charge on mortgages. Each point is equal to 1 percent of the loan amount. Since the buyer can normally deduct points from taxes, your financial advisor may advise you to pay the points in exchange for a lower sales price.

Keep in mind too that if you receive a housing allowance, buy a home, and live in it, you will have some real advantages such as: a choice about where you live; you will be building up equity; you will get an annual tax break not only on the interest and taxes, but an additional break on a housing allowance if such an agreement is arranged with the church in business session or by an appropriate committee in advance.

Also, you will get a tax break, if you follow the same procedure, on the down payment, utilities, and repairs on the house if the deduction does not exceed the fair rental value of the house furnished. In addition to all these benefits, the pastor will be paying on a place to live when retirement comes or if disability should take place. Even if the mortgage debt is never paid off, it's building up a little nest egg of money to either buy a small house or invest the money and use the interest to help rent an apartment.

I realize that the entire amount of the housing allowance is subject to Social Security tax, and that this tax is escalating annually. I know too of the disadvantages in owning your own home when ministers move more frequently than many other professionals. I believe the advantages are worth the risk.

3. What if you own your home now and you are called to a church that has a pastorium and you don't have any choice but to live in it?

(1) I realize that if you sell your home where you presently live without buying another one within two years, at a cost equal to or exceeding that of the sale of the house sold, you will be required to pay capital gains tax on the profit.

But I believe if the Lord leads a pastor to another pastorate and he accepts the church as a part of God's will for his life, the house will not be a negative influence on his accepting that pastorate.

(2) Some pastors who haven't been able to sell their houses when they moved to new pastorates have rented them and let the

monthly rent make the mortgage payments. It may have some drawbacks, but it is being done profitably by many ministers.

My conclusion is simple: if you move into a pastorium, enjoy it and think of the advantages of "an instant place to live without choice." If you get a housing allowance, "Happy House Hunting."

15
Getting a Good Start at the Next Pastorate

Getting a good start in almost anything is a great advantage. The same holds true in the pastorate.

1. Getting Acquainted with Your People.—The first few months ought to be a time to get acquainted with your "new flock." When I moved to my last pastorate, we had a "church roll call" for several months on Sunday mornings. We divided the membership alphabetically into groups of approximately a dozen families. I wrote those families a personal letter and stated that their names would be called individually on a certain Sunday and that they would be asked to stand. The procedure did at least two things: (1) It helped me to put the names and faces together. (2) And after a given length of time, every resident member of that church was recognized.

2. Getting to Know Your Leadership.—Well-planned monthly council or church cabinet meetings with organizational leaders will help a pastor initiate a good program, offer opportunity to delegate responsibility, and develop interpersonal relationships with the leadership.

3. Getting a Good Start with Your Staff.—When a pastor goes to a new pastorate with a staff already present, he needs to establish a good rapport with them. Also, he needs to set up some regular weekly staff meetings. This is a "must." A church will not function properly if the staff is not organized and working as a team in accordance with adequate job descriptions.

4. Getting a Good Beginning as a Leader.—A pastor can get a good start when he demonstrates from the beginning that he is a good leader. Working with others in a decisive and cooperative manner is important. Everyone is human and will make mistakes, but dwelling on failure never leads to success.

5. Getting to Know the Spiritual Gifts of Your People.—A pastor can get a good start by striving to know the spiritual gifts of his members. In every congregation people have various gifts of the Spirit, but many of them have never discovered them. The pastor who is willing to encourage those people to utilize such gifts will build a great fellowship.

6. Getting a Good Schedule.—It is wise to set up some kind of pastoral schedule as soon as possible. This will vary according to each pastor. But setting up some specific hours for study is essential. The pastor who gives the "leftover time" for sermon preparation will not only penalize his members but himself as well.

I like the old Norwegian proverb: "When the crib is empty, the horses bite one another." And when the people are fed, they are more content in the fellowship, and there is less nit-picking among the members.

7. Getting a Good Visitation Program.—Start or continue a good visitation program. Set the example by being a part of it. For years, I set aside every Tuesday evening to visit with the men of the church. We visited the unsaved and the unchurched. Have various times set aside for church members to visit. It doesn't have to be a Tuesday or Thursday night, but the important thing is to contact people with the good news about Jesus Christ and the church.

8. Getting Involved in Ministerial Conferences and Associational Work.—Get to know your fellow ministers. Attend the ministerial and pastors' conferences. Develop a support system. Attend and support your associational or district programs. Be a team member.

Getting a good start in your new ministry can lead a pastor and congregation in an exciting and effective work for the Master.

16
An Installation Service at the New Pastorate

More churches are using some kind of installation service to mark the beginning of a pastor's ministry at a new pastorate. I think this is wise, and I am giving a sample of one you may want to use as a guide at the beginning of your new work.

The installation service may be part of a regular morning or evening worship hour or planned for another specified time. The main purpose of such a service is the mutual dedication and commitment of the pastor and the congregation.

The service of installation given below is a modified order of the one given by the Madison Creek Baptist Church in Goodlettsville, Tennessee, on Sunday afternoon, October 28, 1979, for their new pastor, Reverend James Gordon Monro.

INSTALLATION SERVICE
The Prelude, A Word of Welcome, The Call to Worship, The Invocation, The Scripture Reading (Jer. 1:4-10; 1 Tim. 4:11-16, 2 Tim. 4:1-5), The Anthem, The Sermon, The Statement of the Presiding Minister.

THE COVENANT BETWEEN PEOPLE AND PASTOR
LEADER: Having been called as pastor of _____ Church, will you now reaffirm before these people your faith in God the Father, Creator of all that is, in Jesus Christ as your Lord and Savior, and in the Holy Spirit as your Teacher, and do you take the people of this church to be your people, this community to be your field of labor, without reservation of heart or mind?

PASTOR: I do.

LEADER: Do you promise to give yourself faithfully to the ministry of the Word and to prayer, to be a good shepherd of this flock of God, to minister to the needs of all alike, to be the friend of all who will permit you, to seek always to build up the body of Christ, to share the good news of Jesus Christ in this community and in the whole world, if wronged to forgive as you expect to be forgiven, to keep yourself mentally alert and physically fit, and to lead this church in the ways of Christ as the Holy Spirit may give you wisdom and strength?

PASTOR: I do. I will seek in all ways to act in accordance with God's will as discerned in the scriptures and prayer, mediated by the wisdom of the Christian community, and struggled within the depths of my soul. I gratefully accept the responsibility of pastor of _____ Church and happily join in its mission and ministry in this community and in the whole world. I will faithfully offer the talent, experience, and training I have been given to work with you in the service of our Lord. At the same time, I would lay claim upon your support and guidance that together, we may serve as instruments of God's peace.

LEADER: You have heard from your pastor his willing acceptance of the responsibility he will bear as minister of the gospel in this place. But his role is not a solitary one. It is our heritage that the ministry is shared by all Christians and that the priesthood is for all believers. Therefore, let the members of _____ Church now stand and make its declaration.

Do you confess your faith in God as your Heavenly Father, in Jesus Christ as your Savior and Lord, and in the Holy Spirit as your Teacher? And do you promise, in dependence on divine grace, to serve the Lord and walk in His ways, sharing faithfully and regularly in the worship and service of His church?

MEMBERS OF _____ CHURCH: We do. We now renew our vows of loyalty to our Lord and Savior, Jesus Christ. We willingly covenant together with one another, with our pastor, and with the whole church to extend the gospel in its power and purity into this community and all the earth, to be a church where all are welcome and loved, and from which Christian love is released into the world.

LEADER: (*Prayer*) For the privilege of being followers of Christ and co-workers with His people, for the love, joy, and peace the Spirit brings into our life together, for the acceptance of our lives in service and for the strengthening we receive from Thee.

MEMBERS OF _____ CHURCH: We give thanks, O God, and pray that Thou wilt give us spiritual wisdom to know more of Thee.

CHAIRMAN OF THE DEACONS: As a congregation we have testified to our willingness to support and cooperate with our pastor in every good way. In addition, it is appropriate for us to recognize our special relationship with his family. We now promise to sustain them and love them as our own.

MEMBERS OF _____ CHURCH: And now (give pastor and spouse's name), we receive you warmly into the life of this church. We will laugh with you, weep with you, support and nurture you. We will look to you for an example but will try not to require more than we ought. As we surround you with our love, we set you free to live the lives God has given you.

The Recognition of Guests, The Giving of Greetings, The Hymn, The Benediction.

Part 2
When a Pastor Search
Committee Doesn't Come

17

What Does a Pastor Do When He Is Not Contacted by Another Church?

When I mentioned to one of my pastor friends that I was interested in writing a book about what to do when a pastor search committee comes, he said humorously, "What I want to know is what to do when a committee doesn't come."

My pastor friend's words challenged me. What does a pastor do when a pastor search committee doesn't come, but he wants to leave? Some pastors have repeated contacts by such committees and are asked to consider changing pastorates. But what about those servants of God who are excellent preachers and pastors, but opportunities seldom, if ever, come their way to move to new pastorates? What about the pastor who is having a good ministry at his church but would leave if he had "the right challenge"? Or what about the one who is under severe pressure from the congregation to leave? Should he resign without a place to serve? Or should he keep waiting for that committee that seemingly never comes?

1. Let's take a look at the pastor who is not having contact with pastor search committees, but things are going well at his church. Just be thankful that your ministry is fruitful and that God is greatly blessing your labors. You are probably more fortunate than you realize. Hundreds of pastors would gladly change places with you. They would "love to endure" your successful pastorate! I would say "stay put" and give your very best to your ministry. I could hope that you might follow the suggestions in this material as given in Part 1 on "How to Be Prepared for a Pastor Search Committee" and what will follow in Part 3 on how to have a long pastorate.

You may say, "But I still want to leave even if I am having a good ministry here." I have known many fine pastors over the years who felt they wanted to leave their pastorates. Perhaps they would have left if the right church had opened up, and they had been invited by the pastor search committee to preach there in view of a call. Since that right church did not open up at the right time, did that mean that other churches were not interested in their ministries? Did it mean that they would not have made another church a good pastor? I would say indeed not! Then why did God not open up a new place of service for them?

I wish I could answer this question. Perhaps you are asking the same question right now, "God, why do you not open up another place for me? I want to change churches. I need a new challenge."

The answer may well be: "God wants you right where you are for the present time." He may know quite well that if pastor search committees visited your church and talked with you about leaving that you might be tempted to leave, or even leave. Maybe God is not through with you at your present church. Maybe He has someplace else in store for you at another time, and to leave now might not be God's will.

Another answer could be that you are not ready to go to another church. God may be working on some areas in your life that need changing, and maybe you are not cooperating with His plan. Or it could be possible that you still need to sharpen your skills in certain areas of your ministry, and God knows that if you do not improve those skills you would make the same mistakes at the next place of service. God could be waiting for you to mature in some phases of your ministry before you accept a new challenging work.

It is easy to get discouraged and even bitter when you want to go to another church or ministerial work and "absolutely nothing happens—not even one nibble comes your way." But hang in there, and keep working.

2. What about the pastor who is not having committees and his ministry is *not* going well? Maybe he's miserable because he is having conflict in the church, and he just doesn't know what to do. Furthermore, the conflict is "destructive conflict." Should the

pastor leave to avoid open and overt conflict; or should he stay and fight it out? Are you in this situation in your church?

(1) Before we take a look at some causes of conflict, let's ask, some questions: *What is conflict? Where does it take place? Is it necessary for conflict to take place in the local churches?*

Conflict is a part of everyday living. As Paul Mickey and Robert Wilson say in *Conflict and Resolution:* "Conflict may range from tension between you and your next-door neighbor over his dog digging in your carefully manicured flower bed to the danger of all-out war in the Middle East."[1] And it is increasing all over the world. Yes, it does take place inside the local church, though we would expect it to take place outside the church. Christians have conflict with fellow Christians and pastors have conflicts with fellow church members. Mickey and Wilson say the existence of controversy and conflict inside the church "is highly threatening, because for many people it implies weakness and failure of Christians to live up to the expectations of the gospel."[2] Not all conflict is bad, because if it is handled properly, it may yield positive results. If it is ignored or handled improperly, it may yield devastating results.

It may help pastors to know that change does not initially create reconciliation—but chaos that may lead to conflict. So when too many changes take place in the church, conflict will most likely occur. The pastor will be caught right in the middle of it.

Jesus used conflict as a basic element in His ministry. We only have to read the story of the woman caught in adultery, as recorded in John 8:1-8, to see how Jesus probed into the behavior of those who would have stoned her. Why did the accusers not toss a stone? Because Jesus raised some conflict for them. He asked them to see both sides of the story: their sin as well as hers. He did the same thing when he talked about judging, telling us to get the plank out of our own eye before trying to remove a splinter out of someone else's eye (Matt. 7:3).

So pastors should not be surprised when there is conflict in the church. Reconciliation occurs only as a resolution of conflict. So conflict is not an end in itself but a means toward an end. And negotiation points the pastor and people toward the goal in a conflict situation.

(2) What causes conflict (of the destructive type) in the churches that brings so much tension between the pastors and members? Remember, a church and a pastor cannot grow to any degree when there is fighting taking place between the two. Either the church or the pastor will be on the defensive or on attack—or both.

a. Often the causes are not necessarily the fault of the pastor, but he becomes the scapegoat for things that would have happened even if another pastor had been at that particular church, such as:

● A numerical declining or changing neighborhood or community. This in turn may cause a decline in attendance and offerings.

● Personal conflicts of long standing between members.

● Family power struggles for leadership roles in the church.

● Power struggles between various key people in the church.

● Resentment of new members on the part of the established members because of a growing or changing church membership.

● When the present pastor is compared with a former pastor or pastors concerning his preaching and pastoral style.

● Frequently, a good pastor finds himself in direct conflict with certain members of his church because of a fellow staff member— especially if the staff member has longer tenure at that church. Often a disgruntled church member will use such a staff member "to get to the pastor," especially if previously orchestrated ventures have failed.

● Unknowingly, the pastor may find himself in the midst of longstanding quarrels and hostilities among members that began in prior years because of a "building program" in the church or a bitter fuss over some issue in the public school system. Those old sores may fester time and time again without the pastor even knowing how the hurt got there.

● One of the biggest causes of conflict is the almost impossible expectations placed on the pastor by the members, as already discussed. There is confusion over the role of the pastor. What should he be? What should he do? People have models of ministry. "Why can't our pastor do like the big-city spectacular church pastor or electronic pastor? Why isn't our pastor's record bigger this year than last year?" This creates insecurity for the pastor.

I personally found that many church members want the pastor to have a superabundance of responsibility for the work of the church, but the same people have trouble in defining and assigning much, if any, authority to the pastor.

b. As painful as it may be to accept, other conflicts may be caused by the pastor, directly or indirectly.

• One's interpersonal skills may be extremely weak.

• Sometimes a lack of maturity may cause one to make bad judgments. Often church members are impatient with this kind of pastor when they have for years been accustomed to "a seasoned pastor."

• If a pastor feels insecure, he may become too authoritative to try to compensate for a lack of positive leadership. Or he may find it easier to put the blame for his failures on someone else and totally ignore his own.

• Too often a pastor will not accept his responsibilities as pastor. He does what he wants to do first and just neglects what he does not like to do.

• The incompetence of many pastors is a major cause of conflict. One may "want to preach" but not have the competency to preach. Also, one may "want to be a pastor," but not have the gifts a person needs to be a pastor.

• Laziness is another cause of conflict. The pastor sets his own pace in ministry. He can be industrious or he may choose to loaf.

• The rigidity of some pastors causes terrific conflicts in churches. These pastors haven't learned the meaning of flexibility—the give-and-take in the ministry. They always want to be right, and seldom if ever, admit being wrong about anything.

• The pastor's sin of talking too much and listening too little is a big cause of conflict in many churches. Members will say, "You can't talk to him. He won't listen to anybody. He's just plain stubborn."

• And, of course, some ministers are too sensitive and too defensive, often leading to conflict.

c. A few conflicts between pastors and congregations are brought on because of the pastor's spouse.

● An overaggressive or domineering spouse may bring on conflict between the pastor and congregation.

● Some pastors refuse to admit that this is true. They do not want to cause trouble in their marriage by trying to correct the problem.

● A few pastors temporarily solve this problem by frequent moves to other pastorates.

Some of the causes of conflicts mentioned above need to be taken seriously by pastors lest they lead to involuntary termination. Reconciliation should take place between pastor and people, if at all possible. The pastor needs to take the initiative to set up some kind of evaluation and feedback channels with the congregation. Then, through negotiation, both pastor and people can reach some mutual goals for the unity of the church.

(3) When should a pastor resign? I have talked with a number of pastors who feel like the "destructive conflict" in their churches is so intense they feel led to resign.

When a pastor resigns and leaves his church, he faces two problems: (a) he doesn't have a base from which he can operate so committees can hear him preach, and (b) he must give a full explanation as to why he resigned.

Only on rare occasions or under extremely unusual circumstances should a pastor resign his pulpit without a place to serve or a pulpit to fill. When should a pastor resign:

● When virtually every avenue of exploration has been taken by him to solve whatever seemingly impossible difficulty has caused him to consider resignation, and such avenues of hope have failed. I do not believe many of these "impossible situations" come to a large number of pastors. Certainly not as many of these situations arise as the resignations by so many pastors would lead many to believe. There is a tremendous difference in "staying with in intolerable situation" than there is in "staying with an impossible one." The intolerable one brings severe pain; the impossible one takes more faith to bear the pain.

● When the pastor knows without a doubt that remaining at the church would break his own health or destroy his family relationship.

• When the pastor knows beyond any shadow of a doubt that his ministry has deteriorated to the point he must make the inevitable decision to resign or be involuntarily terminated. Some pastors prefer to take the risk of being terminated with the clear conscience they have done their best to minister to that church rather than running from the place where they knew God led them. The individual pastor himself must determine what is best for him to do. After all, he knows the circumstances better than any other person.

• When friction between the pastor and a large segment of the church has been present over a long period of time and every means of reconciliation has been exhausted between both parties without any appreciable solution.

• When a pastor has become so low spiritually that he really does not care what happens to the church or to himself.

• When the pastor has reached the "burnout" stage, and he is not willing to do anything about it. The burnout stage is the point in a man's ministry where his work becomes a constant strain. It is not the amount of work he does that drains him but the lack of enjoying what he does. The burnout pastor is usually disillusioned, exhausted, depressed, irritable, and overwhelmed. Such a condition may cause sleepless nights or even physical disorders. He often feels trapped. He loses his zestful outlook on life.

The burnout pastor is usually mentally and physically depleted significantly below his normal capable level of ministry. It naturally affects his pastoral work because he begins to complain about his workload and even about his members and associates. He becomes irritated about little things and may get out of touch with his friends and family. He refuses to accept suggestions and worries about what people think of him. And when he cannot meet the unrealistic goals he has set for himself, he gets even more frustrated. Then he becomes apathetic and closes himself off from people who could and want to help him.

The burnout pastor can help himself overcome this dreadful crisis in his life. He must take a good look at himself and defeat the "internal stress." There are other ways to beat the burnout crisis—such as exercise, diet, and relaxation. Find some outside interests. Do not just live, talk, and eat church. Be in control of yourself. A pastor with burnout can overcome this problem. He must want to do so. And if he is not willing to help himself or get help he should not expect the church to suffer with him. Let me suggest that all pastors read Brooks Faulkner's book, *Burnout in Ministry.*[3] He talks about how to recognize it and how to avoid it.

(4) When should a pastor not resign?

● When you are *terribly discouraged.* All pastors have moments when they look for Elijah's juniper tree.

● When you do not feel well, or when you have had an exceedingly difficult week, and "nothing has gone well."

● When you are angry. Wait until you calm down before you make any kind of decision.

● When the budget committee just met, and you know you will not get a raise even though you feel you deserve one.

● When a small group of self-appointed people in your church has talked with you about how bad things are at the church and tried to convince you that if you leave, things would get better.

● When the same little group comes to you later and puts you on a guilt trip by saying, "Pastor, if you don't leave you are going to split the church, and we don't believe you want to be responsible for that."

● When you inherit or secure a staff member who opposes your ministry or refuses to cooperate.

● When somebody says, "Pastor, we love you, but we just think you have been here too long."

● When someone judges your total ministry, regardless of the circumstances, on how many baptisms and additions the church had last year in comparison to what the church had several years ago.

(5) What are some alternatives to resignation?

Many times a pastor will say when he is under pressure to leave, "But I don't have any choice but to leave." That is not necessarily true. There ought to be some alternatives—or at least one might try to find some. Please let me suggest the following:

● If the pastor knows he has a dissident group of people within his fellowship, he ought to take the initiative and try to rebuild a working relationship with them, even if he did not cause the division.

● After the pastor has sought to reestablish some kind of relationship with those who have a conflict with him, he should request them to meet with him to defend himself against any charges that might be brought against him.

● If the group accuses him of poor preaching or the lack of ministerial performance of his stated duties, he ought to agree to improve in the above areas. If other accusations are leveled against him, the pastor would be wise to make the necessary improvements or changes if at all possible. Should the complaints against him be of a petty nature he should at least listen and try to "read between the lines" to discover the actual nonverbal complaints.

● If, after a reasonable length of time, the pastor realizes that the dissident group is not going to cooperate with him, or even try to find a solution to settle their conflicts, he needs to go right on ministering to his congregation. If a pastor resigns every time he has opposition, he will always be in a mood of resignation.

● On the other hand, if a dissident group within the congregation represents a large majority of the membership instead of a minority, and the pastor knows sooner or later that the group may ask for his resignation or even bring it before the entire church congregation for a vote, I personally believe a pastor ought to go before the entire membership and say something along this line: "I realize that many of you feel I should move to another place of service. I know—and you know—that anytime a church votes for a pastor to resign, it hurts both the church and the pastor. I do not believe you want this to happen to your church, or even to me. If you will give me some time, I will make every effort possible to move to another church. I will pray every day for the Holy Spirit to open up the right place of ministry for me. I ask you to join me in this prayer. And even if things improve in our fellowship, I will not look upon that as a sign to remain here." Then I would dismiss the congregation in prayer. *Do not* set a date as to when you will leave.

• Then ask the Holy Spirit to answer your prayer and lead you to a new ministry. You may want to follow some suggestions similar to those listed in this book in the chapter dealing with "Getting a Pastor Search Committee to Visit and/or Hear You Preach."

• Make it clear to the church that you will give them "progress reports" on the contacts you make without naming churches, or people, of course. Keep your word to the membership and do what you tell them. I have known a few pastors to tell their congregations what is mentioned above, and then when things "got better" in the fellowship or when the church experienced one or two unusually good Sundays, the pastor quit looking for a new place of service, and things went from bad to worse. That is not fair to the church. If the church people trust you to keep your word, *keep it.*

(6) What happens if it does come to involuntary termination?

• It may be that after a reasonable amount of time and you are still not relocated that the church will pressure you to resign immediately. What should be the pastor's next step? If you do not have a choice but to resign or to be involuntarily terminated, try to negotiate some terms. As James Massey, secretary of Church Ministers Relations of the Baptist General Association of Virginia, says in his little pamphlet dealing with termination of pastor, *Thirty Days Is Not Enough.* The pastor ought to try to negotiate for at least three to six months with full salary and benefits with the understanding that if he is relocated in another pastorate or a comparable position, the remaining part of the salary and benefits would be discontinued.

You may be thinking right now that negotiation with a church sounds too harsh for God's servant to carry out. Where does the Holy Spirit fit into the process? It may sound harsh, but it is not nearly as harsh as the reality of a pastor and his family being without an income for several months, wondering where they will live and where they will get the next meal.

• In addition to negotiation, you may want to try to talk with someone who has been in the pastorate who has gone through a similar experience. That individual may give some words of wisdom to help you cope with the terrific physical, emotional, mental, financial, and spiritual strain brought on by such a drastic and devastating experience.

● Naturally, you ought to try to get a job outside of the ministry until you are relocated in some ministerially related work such as the pastorate.

● Some of the state conventions now have some financial assistance for terminated ministers, at least on a short-term basis. Contact your convention office and inquire about this assistance.

● You may want to contact the Baptist Sunday School Board in Nashville and look into the possibility of taking a seminar on career assessment. You may find that you may want to consider a new area of ministerial work after taking a good look at your gifts of the Spirit. At the same time, such a study may reinforce your call to the pastorate, and you would be encouraged to ask your friends and others to continue to share your name with churches looking for pastors.

It is my prayer and hope that you may never have to go through the trauma of having to leave your present pastorate without a place to serve. In the event that it should ever happen, I hope the above suggestions will be helpful to you. The words have come out of a heart that cares. I have wept with and prayed for many who have gone through the above experiences. It is not an easy route to travel. I am certainly interested in trying to lighten the load as much as possible.

Part 3
When a Pastor Doesn't Want a Pastor Search Committee to Come

I believe in longer pastorates. Most pastors leave their churches too soon, often to the detriment of their own ministry and the Lord's work. In most instances three years or less (about the average) is too short a pastorate, though I realize there are exceptions.

There are a few situations where a church and a pastor just "click." The congregation wants him to stay indefinitely and he has the same mutual feeling. The church may have periods of growth or maybe even times of decline. But the ministry of both the church and the pastor continue to make a vital contribution to the community and its missionary endeavors reach around the world.

There is deep love between the Lord and the church and also between the pastor and people. Sometimes a pastor may spend his whole ministry at such a church. This does not mean there are never times of "troubled waters" between the pastor and some of the members. Neither does it mean that such a long pastorate is void of conflict between members of the church. Such a church has enough spiritual resilience to stay on the right track and mend its own broken fellowship.

The members know how to forgive one another; also they know how to forgive a pastor when he makes a mistake or fails to measure up to their every expectation. The pastor is secure enough to realize that when a member "gets upset" it may not always be that the member is against him personally—but against what he stands for and who he represents. The people and the pastor both recognize one another's humanity and do not live with grudges and regrets. The pastor himself is a loving and forgiving person with a caring spirit.

18
The Secret or Recipe for a Successful Long Pastorate

I heard Dr. John Laida speak to a group of pastors about some things he would suggest for a long pastorate, things he had practiced in more than twenty years as pastor of the vibrant and growing First Baptist Church of Clarksville, Tennessee. John has given me permission to quote him from the notes I made when I heard his talk. He used 2 Corinthians 5:20 for his Scripture and entitled his remarks: "Guidelines for a Long Pastorate." He gave the following guidelines for a long pastorate:

1. Know that You Are in God's Place and God's Will.

He greatly emphasized the leadership of the Holy Spirit in finding the right place and God's will.

2. Preach the Word.

Magnifying the preaching of God's Word has a central place for every pastor. We can read many books, but there are "66" we must study. John told of a pulpit committee hearing a certain preacher preach on hell and saying, "I don't believe in hell." A member of the committee told him, "If there is not a hell, we don't need a preacher. If there is a hell, we don't need your kind of preaching."

3. Win the Lost.

Pastors must have compassion. This is a must for any kind of pastorate. There is no substitute for winning the lost.

4. Love Your People and Thank Them.

Do not hurt your people. There is a heartache on every pew.

People need encouragement. John said he has written letters of encouragement to people daily, including schoolteachers, Sunday School teachers, and many others.

Thank them for giving—for their stewardship.

Thank them for trying to help you.

Take suggestions from your people, and don't resent it.

Be nice to people.

Lead your people. Don't push them, and don't "beat them to death."

Don't be afraid to ask people to serve.

5. Learn to Delegate Responsibility.

Do not try to do everything by yourself.

Trust your people.

Remember, the pastor is not infallible.

Use your staff, and never double-cross your staff members.

6. Learn to Eat Crow.

When you make a mistake or "goof," tell your people you are sorry and ask for their forgiveness.

The above is a gist of what John Laida said about a long pastorate in the amount of time allotted to him. I believe his suggestions and advice are worth following because God has used him in a remarkable way. What John did not say is that a good, dedicated Christian companion will greatly enhance any pastor's ministry. Dr. Laida has this kind of wife, and her ministry at the church cannot be separated from John's tremendous success in a long pastorate.

In addition to Dr. Laida's foundational remarks, I want to add others that I tried to follow during my pastorates, including my mistakes and blunders:

1. Study and make adequate preparation for the pulpit. It is as unfair to a congregation for a pastor to deliver an unprepared sermon as it is for the preacher to have an unprepared congregation. The pastor who takes shortcuts in preparing his sermons will most likely have a ministry cut short.

There are two basic elements in preaching: preparation and delivery. So the way a preacher prepares his sermons and how he delivers them under the leadership of the Holy Spirit are important:

(1) *Preparation* might fall into several categories.

a. *Textual Sermon.*—This means taking a short Scripture passage (usually a verse or two or maybe even a sentence), thoroughly studying it, and then applying the Scripture to the hearer with the thought of finding some response that will bring a commitment. Various commentaries and "tools" are used for in-depth study.

b. *Expository Sermon.*—This method of preparation is about the same as the textual except the expository sermon deals with several verses of Scripture or even a chapter or book of the Bible. The minister divides these passages into main points or subheads, using a central theme or idea of the passage. He seeks interpretation of the passage in the time in which it was written and how it can be applied to his hearers today. Usually illustrations are used to shed more light on the passage.

c. *Topical Sermon.*—This kind of preparation has characteristics of the textual and expository sermon, but it starts with an idea, a certain topic. It does not deal with any particular passage of Scripture but just elaborates on a subject, biblical or nonbiblical.

(2) *Delivery of the Sermon.* Delivery of the sermon will vary with the individual minister. There are several methods of delivery in preaching:

a. *Extemporaneous Preaching.*—This is the most prevalent method of sermon delivery. The speaker prepares but not to the fullest extent (limited preparation). He organizes his thoughts, but he does not write out his sermon. The language he will use in the sermon will be left to the moment of delivery. He will prepare and use a brief outline (notes) in his preaching. He uses quotations, Scripture references, and illustrations, and relies on his notes to give them.

b. *Reading the Sermon.*—In this method, the minister reads the sermon from a prepared manuscript. Many great and dynamic preachers have used manuscripts such as Jonathan Edwards and John Henry Jowett. In some cases, a minister can read a sermon as freely and effectively as others can preach extemporaneously. But this is rare, and among the average congregation reading sermons is not the most popular form of delivery.

c. *Preaching from Memory.*—This method of delivery differs from the manuscript reader only in that a prepared manuscript is memorized and delivered verbatim without notes. The trouble with this method is that the sermon "sounds" memorized—like it is canned.

d. *Free Delivery Preaching.*—In this method, the preacher prepares a full manuscript, becomes completely familiar with it, then delivers it without notes (one does not memorize it). This is the method I have used since 1950 when I read Clarence Macartney's book, *Preaching Without Notes.*

Preachers usually choose the method of delivery with which they feel most comfortable. They should not be judged by the method someone else uses. The important thing is for God's message to be proclaimed by a servant of God whose character is godly and who is empowered by the Holy Spirit. (I know about one church that dismissed its pastor because he used notes in delivering his sermon. This is foolish and unfair.)

Also, I believe the preparation and delivery of good preaching involves good planning. Utilizing someone else's sermon outlines week after week without in-depth Bible study will produce "weak sermons." It is all right to make use of other people's sermons and resources, but without personalizing such materials a pastor ought to think of the ethics involved in such constant plagiarism. Planned preaching, whether by the month or the year, will help a pastor to avoid "Saturday-night specials."

If or when you repeat any of your sermons to the same congregation, rework them and make them fresh and vital. Always list the sources you use in preparing sermons and reread these as parallel reading to reinforce your thoughts.

2. Spend a lot of time in prayer. One of the biggest regrets I have of my ministry is not saying to several people who came to me with complaints and criticism about the church, "Joe . . . Bill . . . Sue . . . let's talk to the Lord about this situation. It's too big for us to handle."

James Gregg, former director of the Tennessee Baptist Childrens' Homes spoke in chapel at the Tennessee Baptist Convention Executive Board meeting one morning. I recall an incident he mentioned that emphasizes what I am trying to say about prayer. He said when he was in college, a fellow ministerial student was out in his yard one fall day raking leaves and picking up broken limbs and sticks. His little three-year-old girl was helping him. They would both pick up sticks, break them over their knees, and put them in the wheelbarrow to haul away. His little girl picked up one that was too big for her to break, and she said, "Here, Daddy, this one is too big for me to take. You'll have to take care of this one."

Dr. Gregg said about three weeks after that incident, the little three-year-old girl died. The father got very bitter and resentful, and he could not sleep or eat. He grieved day and night. One night when he couldn't sleep, he thought he heard his little girl's voice out of the darkness say, "Here, Daddy, this one is too big for me to take. You'll have to take care of this one." Then that father realized how foolish he had been. He lifted his voice to God in prayer and said, "Oh, God, this burden is too big for me too, Lord. You'll have to take this one." And God lifted his burden and gave him peace and comfort.

If a pastor stays long in a church, he will come to the place many times where he will be compelled to say, "Lord, this problem is too big for me. You will have to handle this one." Yes, prayer is a necessity for God's servant in the pastorate.

3. Always stay positive in your attitudes and actions. People enjoy being around positive and straightforward people. The pastor is God's encourager and enabler. If we become sour and negative, it will reflect in our preaching and in our programs.

4. Keep your enthusiasm. There is not any work in the world that gives more satisfaction and brings more thrill than the pastorate. But it is easy for a pastor to get in a spiritual or ecclesiastical rut with the daily routine of hospital visits, sermon preparation, and administrative affairs. One has to be extremely careful to keep a proper amount of enthusiasm.

5. Do not neglect your family. Take time to be a good companion and parent. Try to take your spouse out to a meal at least once a week. Play with the children. Listen to their complaints and rejoice with them in their achievements. If your family gets discouraged, it will discourage you. The grass wouldn't look nearly so green on another church field if pastors would find more happiness at home. It is very difficult to bring happiness to other families if you neglect your own.

6. Take some time off from your busy schedule. Seven days a week does indeed make one weak. And this weakness has a way

of taking its toll on the emotional, mental, physical, and spiritual energy of a pastor.

7. Keep up with current events. I heard one man brag about the fact that he never used anything but biblical illustrations. It is commendable for a preacher to be able to use these glorious windows in the building of a sermon. But also letting in a little current light will enhance the great old truths.

8. Keep adding good books to your library. Take time to read them and use them.

9. Take advantage of theological seminars, Bible study conferences, pastor's schools and retreats, church administration, and other good seminars.

10. Take annual vacations. Pastors who brag about never taking vacations are not helping their churches, families, or themselves. Every pastor needs to "just get away from it all" for a few days every year.

11. Learn how to take criticism: constructive and destructive. I realize it is easier to take the first than it is the latter. More than twenty years ago, I had come back to my motel room following a revival meeting and late dinner engagement in one member's home near Chattanooga, Tennessee. Doris Day, the movie star, was being interviewed on a late evening television program. She was asked a simple question: "Doris, what was the hardest thing you had to learn in show biz?" said the interviewer. She pondered just a moment and said, "The hardest thing I had to learn in show biz is that everybody is not going to love you and like you." This is true in the pastorate. And the sooner pastors learn it, the less stress they will endure. Remember, everybody did not like our Lord. He kept loving them and turned to those who would accept His help.

12. Do not develop a martyr's complex. Do not look for trouble and then rejoice that you found it. Neither should a pastor minister with the feeling that he will become more spiritual if he is persecuted, criticized, or mistreated.

13. Have a healthy attitude toward your fellow ministers. Make some of them part of your support system. Avoid petty jealousies. Never try to compare your gifts of the Spirit with your peer group.

You are accountable to God for how you use what He has given you.

Long pastorates mean a lot of give-and-take, an abundance of love for your members, and a great deal of good old hard work. The joys of watching the children grow up and observing the spiritual maturity of the saints God gives every pastor to oversee is worth the extra time and effort.

Conclusion

In the preceding pages, I have tried to take my pastor friends on a pilgrimage in the area of dealing with a pastor search committee. You will notice that I began with how to get ready for such a committee and tried to take the prospect right up to the call, the vote, and the beginning in a new pastorate. In case a committee didn't come, I have discussed how you can deal with your present pastorate or what happens if you must resign. If things are going great, I made suggestions about how to have a long pastorate.

In the introductory section, I stated very clearly that there never will be two ministers just alike, and no two ministers will approach the matter of dealing with a pastor search committee in the same manner and style.

I made the remarks about ministers dealing with the pastor search committees with different approaches and styles because I realize that what works for one pastor may not necessarily work for another. Consequently, even though I believe the suggestions are valid and have worked in the past for other ministers, I urge you to use your discretion and best judgment in using this material.

All prescriptions have some "side effects." That's why some medicines will relieve or heal many patients but cause complications in the bodies of others. Like the physicians would admit, it's difficult to know who is allergic to certain drugs until the patient tries them. I'm positive, beyond any doubt, that I'm allergic to penicillin because one injection almost took my life in 1959. But for others, the same drug is a "wonder drug" and does magic against certain types of infection in the body.

I am positive about one thing with pastors dealing with pastor search committees: too many ministers are apparently using the wrong prescriptions, or too many pastor search committee members are giving out poor instructions because there are too many side effects. Too many pastors are getting hurt; too many churches are getting sick. There must be a better way to improve the prescriptions on the part of the committees and the ministers. That is why I have tried to write out some improvements over a system that must not be working as well as it should.

In the book, I have repeatedly emphasized that the Great Physician is the One who has the first and last authority to bring a pastor and a search committee together. His prescription, when followed, will never leave any side effects. But He uses human instruments to dispense the right ingredients. God never uses "magic" to bring a pastor and a church together. That's why I believe God uses so many sources (like resumés, pastors, schools, directors of missions, state conventions, and others) to bring the pastors and churches together as a team.

I do have some concluding suggestions to help my pastor friends have a better ministry.

● With the large supply of clergy in some denominations, pastors may stay longer in their present pastorates. It will not be as easy to move from one church to another as it was back in the fifties. So put your roots down deeper, and don't plan to be as mobile as some may want to be.

● Work harder in building up a good "support system" in your pastorate. Don't be a "loner." People need people. Find a good friend or friends you can trust and "pour out your heart" to. I had a friend like that at my last pastorate, and we had a lot of cups of coffee together and prayed together. My friend was Dr. Howard Olive, a neighboring pastor. I still look upon him as "Mr. Integrity." Or perhaps you have need of a "small-group" support system. But like Jesus, surround yourself with friends.

● In discussing the "burnout" stage in Part 2, I said the minister must take a good look at himself and defeat the "internal stress." And then I mentioned the need for exercise, diet, and relaxation to beat this inner stress—this "burnout"—in a person's ministry.

Looking at my own ministry, past and present, I'm more convinced now than ever that these three things are a *necessity* in ministry. Ministers do not get enough of the right kind of exercise. And without it, you cannot feel your best. Ministers need some kind of regular routine exercise. Once a week will not do it. It should be done at least three times a week, and it is better to exercise at approximately the same time each day. I have found that using a stationary bicycle and then walking and running for at least twenty minutes a day really helps. It helps keep your weight down, too, especially the running. A minister cannot feel as well without some kind of planned exercise, whether it be golf or chopping wood. Choose the exercise that suits you, but exercise.

Most ministers probably do not keep their weight at the recommended level according to their age and height. Overweight can cause hypertension and other physical problems.

Relaxation is another "must" for pastors. The body was not made to go at full speed seven days a week. And, with the heavy load the average minister must carry emotionally, mentally, and spiritually, periods of relaxation are necessary.

Pastor, have you had this experience: One evening in one of my pastorates when my boys were young, I was at home one Thursday evening relaxing and reading before an open fire in the fireplace. Suddenly I had this strange feeling. What am I doing home with my family? What meeting have I missed? My guilt so overwhelmed me that I got up out of the easy chair and went to another room to check my appointment book to see what I had missed and why I was at home. I knew I didn't have an appointment before I checked that book. But I looked in spite of what I knew. Why did I do it? I deserved that time at home with my family. I needed that relaxation. Pastor, learn how to relax and enjoy it. You need it. You'll be a better minister.

● Be aware of certain stages in your ministry so you can take extra caution and not become a "ministerial casualty." Some call them crises in ministers' lives. There are three of them in particular: The first stage is the first five years of ministry. The young pastor, having been called early in life, has spent most of his life in schools. He has read a lot of books and taken a lot of exams.

But when he gets out in the pastoral field it's quite different from the classroom. Now he comes face-to-face with people and problems, and his courses of study didn't prepare him for these interpersonal relationships. After about three to five years, he begins to ask himself some questions: Am I really in the right vocation? Should I stay or leave? Will it always be like this? Are all the churches like this one? And unless he has the tenacity to "take it," he may be tempted to throw in the towel and walk out.

The second stage comes around forty years of age. And he still has some questions: Will the next twenty years be about the same as the last ones? Is this really what I want to do for the next two decades? What will my next church be like, or have I gone about as far as I can go? And have I, in my ministry, reached the point of no return? Some leave the ministry at this point, especially if a pastor search committee doesn't come. Others keep waiting to move on to more fruitful opportunities of ministry.

The last stage, or crisis, comes at about age sixty or sixty-five, the time to retire. Most ministers are not prepared for retirement, financially or emotionally. Fortunately many churches now have some kind of annuity plans, and there is Social Security. Just as it is difficult to really get into the ministry during that first stage it is likewise difficult to get out in the last one. Some men even retire earlier than sixty-five, knowing that they are not ready to live on what they have earned in the ministry. Some hope a part-time job plus their small church annuity and Social Security will see them through their retirement days.

When pastors realize these crises (or stages) will most likely take place in their lives, they can be better prepared to face them and stay in the ministry—and perhaps keep waiting for that pastor search committee.

● In recent days, because of so much destructive conflict in so many churches, I have heard many pastors say, "There's something wrong with our system." Yes, when many pastor search committees limit their search to pastors under fifty years of age, there is a tendency to make such remarks. Pastors fifty years and older often have their most productive ministries. And I have experienced many fine churches turning to older men. But as long as the church to which you belong has the "open" or "restricted-open" method of calling a pastor, you simply learn to live with it. The method, in spite of some drawbacks, has a lot of pluses, a lot of advantages. And I'm glad my ministry has been under such a system. I hope you feel the same way.

If you are looking for a pastor search committee, I hope it comes your way. I pray that God will lead you to the right church. If one doesn't come, hang in there, and do your best for the One who called you to minister.

Notes

Introduction
1. This means the congregation is free to call whomever it wishes as pastor.

Chapter 2
1. Robert D. Dale, *My Ministry Here Is Completed:* or *How to Write a Resume Right,* page 1 on paper mimeographed for Southeastern Baptist Theological Seminary Students (6 pages).
2. Ibid.

Chapter 8
1. Lucille Lavender, *They Cry Too* (New York: Hawthorn Books, Inc., 1976).
2. Jackson W. Carroll and Robert L. Wilson, *Too Many Pastors?* (New York: The Pilgrim Press, 1980), p. 36.
3. Ibid., p. 37.
4. Ibid.

Chapter 9
1. James D. Glasse, *Putting It Together in the Parrish* (Nashville: Abingdon Press, 1972), p. 19.
2. Ibid., p. 18.
3. Ibid., p. 20.
4. Ibid., p. 33.
5. Lyle E. Schaller, *The Pastor and the People: Building a New Partnership for Effective Ministry* (New York and Nashville: Abingdon Press, 1973), p. 20.

Chapter 17
1. Paul A. Mickey and Robert L. Wilson, *Conflict and Resolution* (Nashville: Abingdon Press, 1973), p. 9.
2. Ibid., pp. 9-10.
3. Brooks R. Faulkner, *Burnout in Ministry* (Nashville: Broadman Press, 1981).

Bibliography

Blakemore, James H. *A Preacher's Temptations.* Raleigh: Edwards & Broughton Company, 1966.

Bratcher, Edward B. *The Walk-on-Water Syndrome.* Waco: Word, Inc., 1984.

Brister, C. W., Cooper, James L., and Fite, J. David. *Beginning Your Ministry.* Nashville: Abingdon Press, 1981.

Brown, Jerry W. *Church Staff Teams that Win.* Nashville: Convention Press, 1979.

Carroll, Jackson W. and Wilson, Robert L. *Too Many Pastors?* New York: The Pilgrim Press, 1980.

Collins, Gary, *You Can Profit from Stress.* Santa Ana: Vision House Publishers, 1977.

Dale, Robert D. *Growing a Loving Church.* Nashville: Convention Press, 1974.

Faulkner, Brooks R. *Getting on Top of Your Work.* Nashville: Convention Press, 1973.

_____. *Burnout in Ministry.* Nashville: Broadman Press, 1981.

_____. et al. *Stress in the Life of the Minister.* Nashville: Convention Press, 1981.

Glasse, James D. *Putting It Together in the Parish.* Nashville: Abingdon Press, 1972.

Hahn, Celia A. *The Minister Is Leaving.* New York: The Seabury Press, 1974.

Howse, W. L. *The Church Staff and Its Work.* Nashville: Broadman Press, 1959.

Johnson, Joe. *"Preacher, You're the Best Pasture We've Ever Had!"* Nashville: Broadman Press, 1972.

Kennedy, Gerald. *The Seven Worlds of the Minister.* New York, Evanston, and London: Harper & Row, 1968.

Lavender, Lucille. *They Cry Too!* New York: Hawthorn Books, Inc., 1976.

MacGorman, Jack W. *The Gifts of the Spirit.* Nashville: Broadman Press, 1974.

McBurney, Louis. *Every Pastor Needs a Pastor.* Waco: Word, Inc., 1977.

Meiburg, Albert L. *Called to Minister.* Nashville: Convention Press, 1968.

Mickey, Paul A. and Wilson, Robert L. *Conflict & Resolution.* Nashville: Abingdon Press, 1973.

Montgomery, Felix E. *Pursuing God's Call: Choosing a Vocation in Ministry.* Nashville: Convention Press, 1981.

Mosley, Ernest E. *Priorities in Ministry.* Nashville: Convention Press, 1978.

Osborne, Cecil. *The Art of Understanding Yourself.* Grand Rapids: Zondervan Publishing House, 1967.

Schaller, Lyle E. *The Pastor and the People.* Nashville: Abingdon Press, 1973.

————. *Parish Planning.* Nashville: Abingdon Press, 1971.

————. *The Local Church Looks to the Future.* Nashville: Abingdon Press, 1968.

Shoemaker, Samuel M. *Beginning Your Ministry.* New York, Evanston, and London: Harper & Row, Publishers, 1963.

Sparks, James Allen. *Pot-Shots at the Preacher.* Nashville: Abingdon Press, 1977.

Turnbull, Ralph G. *A Minister's Obstacles.* Westwood: Fleming H. Revell Company, 1944.

Wedel, Leonard E. *Building & Maintaining a Church Staff.* Nashville: Broadman Press, 1966.